IMMANUEL, GOD WITH US

IMMANUEL, GOD WITH US

A daily devotional counting down 100 days to Christmas

By Ron Barnard

First Printing: 2014

ISBN 978-1-312-35920-8

Produced by Leah Bussert
Illustrations by Greg Pampell

Published by Ron Barnard
P.O. Box 3395 Wilmington, NC 28406

www.thesamnetwork.com

To Mom and Dad:

Thanks for making Christmas special no matter what we had and for teaching me Immanuel is always with us.

FOREWORD

I have been married to "Mr. Christmas", as Ron has been affectionately nicknamed, for 26 years. In all honesty, he has at times overwhelmed me with his love of the Christmas season. I wouldn't call myself a scrooge, but I'm certainly NOT "Mrs. Christmas" either. Over the years, however, I have learned to be thankful for the foundation of faith Ron has established in our home through his strongly held belief that God, "Immanuel," is always with us. God desires to be near and intimately involved in our lives on the good days and the difficult days. I believe He especially wants us to know He's near on the days when we feel alone and empty.

The Christmas season can be difficult for a variety of reasons, the crazy schedules, expectations of others, or the emptiness created by the absence of those to whom we have had to say "Goodbye." These have been very real challenges that at times have made it hard for me to focus on the true meaning of the season. I'm thankful for eternity. I'm also thankful we can anchor our hope in "Immanuel" knowing in the deepest part of our hearts that we can bring all our cares to Him, because He cares for us (1 Peter 5:7).

This book is written in such a way that most of the devotionals are stand-alone readings. Let it serve as an inspiration and resource. It's OK if you skip around. Show yourself some grace and focus your time more on meditating on the truth of what you read, rather than just trying to get through them all.

Thank you for making the choice to pick up this book. The fact that you are reading it represents to me an investment of time and money as well as a personal desire to invest in your own journey of faith. I pray it will prove a good investment and that in these pages you will find hope, encouragement, and supernatural joy, as you embark on this and every future Christmas season.

Breathe in and breathe out, and keep putting one foot in front of the other. Let this be a part of your journey toward learning what it means to walk out your faith with Immanuel. And remember, you never walk alone…

-Karen Barnard

SEPTEMBER

100 DAYS UNTIL CHRISTMAS

Matthew 1:23 (NIV) "Behold, the virgin shall conceive and bear a son, and they shall call his name Immanuel (which means, God with us)."

I originally started the Countdown to Christmas devotional as a daily blog. I wrote while traveling on mission both stateside and overseas in southern Africa. I wrote from home, sitting in coffee shops, airports, hotels, guesthouses, friend's houses, and even in the African bush. Some of the devotions read a bit like a journal entry and were left as such because of the uniqueness of that day. Others were written in specific response to the day's events or news. They are all meant as a not so subtle reminder of who Christmas is about.

I've long been known for counting down the days until Christmas to the joy of some and the polite annoyance of others. I know Christmas can be hectic and even heavy, especially if you've experienced crisis or tragedy. It was this awareness and the personal tragedies of some of our special friends that caused me to write in the first place. Of course, it's not so much Christmas that I wrote about, but rather the Christ of Christmas, Immanuel, God with us.

The perspectives shared are from a life lived in the reality of His faithfulness and presence. Like everyone else, I've experienced bad and good, hurt and healing, battle and blessing. I talk about them all in this daily discourse. What I've found to be true and what I testify to here, is that in all of that Immanuel is always with us. His presence is predetermined, not conditional. He's with us when it's good and He's with us when it's not. Granted, there are times when it's more difficult to see or feel His nearness, but nonetheless He is here and He is near. "The Word became flesh and walked among us." He still does. "I will never leave you or forsake you"

I have no issue with Christmas music, lights, trees or presents. In fact, I enjoy them all. But at the end of it Christmas is about one thing. Christmas is about a God who left heaven and came to earth. He came to redeem and deliver. He came to live and to ultimately die. In coming he overcame death and the grave. He paid sin's price and broke sin's curse. With less fanfare than we can imagine the King of creation entered this world so we could be delivered from it. He is Immanuel, God with us.

FAITHFUL IN BATTLE

Immanuel is God with us. Not God was with us, or will be with us, but has always been, and always will be with us. That's Faithfulness.

I'm not saying things always go the way we wish they would. In fact, they often don't. What I am saying is that even then God is faithful. It's His faithfulness to be with us that inspires and anchors our lives.

1 Corinthians 1:9 (NIV) “God, who has called you into fellowship with his Son Jesus Christ our Lord, is faithful.”

The Greek word for faithfulness is *pistis* {pis'-tis}, and is used to describe the quality of "fidelity", or "reliability." It is “the character of one who can be relied on..." (Thayer’s Greek Lexicon). William Barclay calls it "the virtue of reliability".

Lamentations 3:22 (NLT) “The unfailing love of the LORD never ends. By his mercies we have been kept from complete destruction. Great is his faithfulness; his mercies begin afresh each day. I say to myself, ‘The LORD is my inheritance; therefore, I will hope in him.’ The LORD is wonderfully good to those who wait for him and seek him. So it is good to wait quietly for salvation from the LORD.”

God is faithful on so many levels. Certainly, He is faithful in battle. That’s good news since we face battles every day. The battles we face come in all shapes and sizes, some are external and some are internal. We face battles of the heart and battles of the mind, physical and spiritual.

Just so you know, you’re not the first to face a fight. Consider Gideon’s story, or maybe check with Joshua or Caleb. Paul could no doubt give a quick discourse on the consistency of being contested. You might also check with Jehoshaphat or a number of the other kings and prophets from the Bible who fought the good fight. But if you still need a witness, there’s always David.

David was only a boy when he faced and defeated the Philistine, yet even at his young age he was destined to be a victor and a king. Goliath wasn’t just a full size soldier. He was a giant! His breastplate weighed 125 pounds, and the tip of his spear weighed between 15-25 pounds. This giant of a man had haunted and taunted an army and a nation.

Yet we know that in 1 Samuel 17, God gave David one of the greatest upset victories in history. The minute David put his faith in God, Goliath became the underdog.

What giants are you facing today? What in your past or present haunts you? What trouble, trial, or challenge stands between you and your destiny?

Whatever the case, remember you don't fight alone. Immanuel is God with us and He is faithful in battle.

FAITHFUL AT DEAD ENDS

Have you ever found yourself at a dead end? I'm a bit of a directional driver, which means I assume that a road pointed in the right direction will lead to my intended destination. Of course, not all roads go through. More than once I've ended up in a cul-de-sac or at the end of a street with no way out and I have to reverse or make a U-turn. Life has its own dead ends: relationships that went nowhere, big deals in business that didn't go through, a career path or plan that didn't work out, illness, hardship, or loss. These are difficult dead ends for sure!

The story of Moses reveals the presence and faithfulness of God at what could only be described as a journey with dead end after dead end. To begin with, Moses was born into captivity and at a time when Pharaoh had ordered the murder of every newborn Jewish boy. Pharaoh feared the Jews were becoming too numerous and would soon be a threat to their Egyptian overlords. Ironically, God not only delivered Moses from death, but into the house of the very man who had intended his destruction.

But the story doesn't END there. I have a feeling Moses would say his situation went from bad, to good, to bad again. One hastily-made choice banished Moses from Pharaoh's palace to the far side of the desert.

Exodus 2:11-12, 15 (NIV) "One day, after Moses had grown up, he went out to where his own people were and watched them at their hard labor. He saw an Egyptian beating a Hebrew, one of his own people. Looking this way and that and seeing no one, he killed the Egyptian and hid him in the sand…When Pharaoh heard of this, he tried to kill Moses, but Moses fled from Pharaoh and went to live in Midian, where he sat down by a well."

FYI, Midian would have been listed in Rand McNally under desert destinations. Talk about the proverbial dead end! I'm sure at this point Moses must have been thinking whatever good he could have done was undone! Of course, what Moses didn't know was that God was at work on the very deliverance Pharaoh had feared. Moses found favor in Midian, and he found favor with God. How astonished Moses must have been when after a 40 year wait God spoke to him through a burning bush in the desert, revealing a process and plan for Moses's restoration and his people's deliverance. It turns out a dead end can be a great place to see and hear from God.

Exodus 3:9-10 (NIV) "The cries of the people of Israel have reached me, and I have seen how the Egyptians have oppressed them with heavy tasks. Now go, for I am sending you to Pharaoh. You will lead my people, the Israelites, out of Egypt."

What appeared to be a dead end turned out to be a redemptive preparation for the very thing Moses was called to be and do. At 40 years of age Moses was a city boy, ill equipped for a wilderness evacuation. At 80 he knew his way around a desert, and he knew the faithfulness of God.

Moses would face many more obstacles on his journey. The obstinate Pharaoh, the Red Sea, the scarcity of food and water in the wilderness, and the disobedient people he was called to lead, were each a dead end in their own right.

Certainly, we face dead ends too. Maybe you are at a dead end even now. Take courage and remember as Moses did, Immanuel, God with us, is faithful even at "dead ends."

ALWAYS WITH US

Psalm 8:3-4 (NIV) "When I consider Your heavens, the work of Your fingers, the moon and the stars, which You have ordained, What is man that You are mindful of him, and the son of man that You visit him?"

Life has a way of making us feel forgotten. I'm sure when Moses was in the Midian desert, he thought God had forgotten him. When David was on the run from Saul, or when Joseph was thrown into prison for doing what was right, they may have thought God had lost their number too.

I've felt that way myself. There have been times when what I knew was true didn't match the emotion of the moment. Pain, problems, letdown or even loss can push the peace of His presence to the margins of our awareness in a quick minute. It's easy to assume when life goes hard that God is gone. Even if we don't believe that lie, we may still struggle with how we feel. As they say, "perception is often greater than reality." The emotion that accompanies difficulty can make us feel forgotten.

But the real truth is that God is faithfully present and aware. You're not missing and He's not absent. Choosing to believe that takes a faith in His Faithfulness and a belief in His character that supersedes our emotions, and goes beyond how we feel.

You're the very reason He came in the first place. The baby in the manger is a not so subtle reminder that we are not forgotten and we are not alone. Immanuel is always with us, and always aware.

Matthew 10:29-31 "Are not two sparrows sold for a penny? And not one of them will fall to the ground apart from your Father. But even the hairs of your head are all numbered. Fear not, therefore; you are of more value than many sparrows."

SUPERNATURAL SPECIALIST

Did you ever think about how specialized our world has become?

When we have a medical issue we turn to a medical professional, not a mechanic. Conversely, if you're having a problem with your car you're not likely to call a cardiac clinic.

We even have different doctors or specialists within the medical profession. You'd never go to an optometrist for digestive difficulties. We have specialist in other fields as well. Mechanical, electrical, chemical, construction, and biomedical are all different types of engineers, and none of them work for the railroad.

We have specialty stores for specialty products, special schools for specific types of learning, and restaurants, don't even get me started...

But here's a cool and important revelation about "Immanuel, GOD with us." He's always exactly who we need in every situation.

When it comes to everything life and living, Jesus is the one and only, and the only God you'll ever need. His power, wisdom, and understanding, are exactly what we need no matter what we're facing.

Jeremiah 51:15 "It is he who made the earth by his power, who established the world by his wisdom, and by his understanding stretched out the heavens."

Let's be clear, no one can be God for you but God. That's why I'm thankful we have GOD with us, He supernaturally specializes in everything.

POWER OF PRESENCE

Today I spent some time chatting to someone walking through a very difficult physical struggle. It was the kind of challenge or struggle that not only threatens to reduce the quality-of-life, but that threatens life itself, at least on this side of eternity.

It's not a new conversation; in fact, it's all too common. If you've been alive for more than a minute, you have endured difficulty and trouble. Maybe you are even now.

Jesus said, "In the world you will have trouble. But take heart; I have overcome the world." John 16:33 (NIV)

Take heart? How?

Take heart in knowing God has overcome and - He has come - so we can overcome!

It's called the power of presence, and when you're in trouble nothing is more important than presence!

There may have been times when your heart was heavy and what you needed was someone to sit with you. You didn't need someone to try to explain things that no one is certain of, or try to rationalize the hurt that can't be explained away. You just needed someone to be there through the pain, and to hold onto you so you could hold onto hope.

FYI, no one does that the way Jesus can and does. That's why they called Him Immanuel.

Psalms 16:11 (NLT) "You will show me the way of life, granting me the joy of your presence and the pleasures of living with you forever."

Hebrews 13:5 "... for he has said, "I will never leave you nor forsake you."

THE TROUBLE WITH TROUBLE

Trouble is one very common reality.

Someone once said that if Moses were coming down from Mt. Sinai today carrying two tablets, they might well be aspirin. Problems are a problem we all deal with.

We know problems and trouble are relative. As soon as we think ours is the worst, we see someone else who is experiencing even more.

My pain levels are consistently high and challenge me every day. Yet, I know there are those who deal with immeasurably more significant and debilitating pain!

Still, that reality doesn't make my pain or yours any less.

Again, Jesus said, "In the world you will have trouble. But take heart; I have overcome the world" (John 16:33).

Trouble is real, and often very difficult to cope with.

In yesterday's devotional, we were reminded of the power of presence. Today, I want to remind you that however real your trouble is, His presence is even more real.

Whatever your trouble, it's likely and reasonably significant to you; and it's significant to Jesus as well!

Matthew 10:29 – 31 (NKJV) "What is the price of two sparrows—one copper coin? But not a single sparrow can fall to the ground without your Father knowing it. And the very hairs on your head are all numbered. So don't be afraid; you are more valuable to God than a whole flock of sparrows."

However great the shadow of the Fall, the shadow of the cross, and the redemption and healing it brings, is even greater!

The key to lifting a head that's down is a heart that's looking up.

Psalms 121:1-2 "I lift up my eyes to the hills. From where does my help come? My help comes from the Lord, who made heaven and earth."

FAITH OR OPTIMISM?

Hope... does it come from a confidence you have in God or is it simply the result of optimism?

If your hope is the result of optimism, you may not feel very hopeful when your situation takes a negative turn. The most difficult situations can take away your ability to be optimistic.

Don't get me wrong, I like optimistic people, and I am one!

However, life often deals us a hand with which, from any temporal perspective, we simply cannot win, no matter how we play it.

Optimism, like any other human attempt at hope, will always find itself, at some point, over-matched by reality.

Faith, on the other hand, transcends and overcomes what we see and feel! It takes us beyond reality to the supernatural place of grace where hope can coexist with hurt. Faith can ultimately bring healing from hurt!

An optimist might say, "I'm optimistic about my situation," where a person of faith would say, "I'm trusting in the nature and character of my God."

The one is circumstantial the other is certain!

Faith opens our eyes to the hope that otherwise we could never even optimistically see.

2 Kings 6:15 – 17 (NASB) "Now when the attendant of the man of God had risen early and gone out, behold, an army with horses and chariots was circling the city. And his servant said to him, "Alas, my master! What shall we do?" So he answered, "Do not fear, for those who are with us are more than those who are with them." Then Elisha prayed and said, "O LORD, I pray, open his eyes that he may see." And the LORD opened the servant's eyes and he saw; and behold, the mountain was full of horses and chariots of fire all around Elisha."

Faith allows us to "see" that GOD is always with us.

HOPE FOR HUMPTY, PART 1

Psalms 147:3 “He heals the brokenhearted and binds up their wounds.”

Humpty Dumpty sat on a wall,

Humpty Dumpty had a great fall.

All the king's horses and all the king's men

Couldn't put Humpty together again.

Who ever heard of horses that could put an egg back together? Seriously, how could those hooves have aided in egg reconstruction? It wasn’t just the horses that weren’t up to the task either. The king’s men were no more effective than his horses. Hands may have been less awkward but they were no more able than hooves to reverse the effects of the fall.

What's true for eggs is true for people too. The fall has had a dramatic and very negative impact on our world and on our lives. Romans 5:12 says “Therefore, just as sin came into the world through one man, and death through sin, and so death spread to all men because all sinned.”

As with Humpty Dumpty, we need look no further than the fall for an explanation of our brokenness. If you watch the morning news or listen to the latest political/cultural debate in our world, you will know this world is broken. We are all impacted by it and none of us are without personal responsibility for it.

Romans 3:23 – “For all have sinned and fall short of the glory of God.”

We’ve all suffered from the result of our own choices and from the choices of others. But then that's why the King came. Yeah, you heard me right, the King came! Turns out He didn't leave the job of fixing broken people to horses or men!

Immanuel, God with us, is the King who came for us! He didn’t do away with sin’s penalty; but rather, He paid it!

Romans 5:19 “For as by the one man's disobedience the many were made sinners, so by the one man's obedience the many will be made righteous.”

Romans 6:23 “For the wages of sin is death, but the free gift of God is eternal life in Christ Jesus our Lord.”

That “life” starts the minute we look to Immanuel. Nearness was necessary for our healing and so, He came. He came to do what only He could!

Psalm 34:18 “The Lord is near to the brokenhearted and saves the crushed in spirit.”

If your spirit is crushed or your heart is broken, it need not stay that way. Know that He is near. Choose repentance over regret, forgiveness over bitterness, and healing rather than holding onto hurt! When you do, know that He will heal you!

He allows us to play a part in His work of restoration, like a carefully crafted instrument in the hand of the great physician, but it is He and only He who is the healer. It’s not the work of horses or men but the hand of our Father King that “heals the brokenhearted.” That’s why He came. Immanuel, God with us.

HOPE FOR HUMPTY, PART 2

Job 42:10 “And the LORD restored the fortunes of Job, when he had prayed for his friends. And the LORD gave Job twice as much as he had before.”

Humpty Dumpty sat on a wall,

Humpty Dumpty had a great fall.

All the king's horses and all the king's men

Couldn't put Humpty together again.

What was Humpty thinking, an oversized egg, sitting on the edge of a tall wall? It seems a bit risky, to say the least. After all, Proverbs 16:18 says, Pride goes before destruction, and a haughty spirit before a fall. Surely, Humpty’s mom had warned him to keep away from edges and ledges, lest he end up a scrambled egg. Yet, this hardboiled head case proudly put himself in danger.

But hold on, here’s another possibility, an alternate theory to this tragedy. What if Humpty was pushed?

Maybe the fall wasn't Humpty's fault at all. In the same way, life is not only the result of what has been done by us, but what has been done to us. One thing is for certain. Life is fragile. Circumstances and situations can seem to crush us beneath the weight of worry, unmet expectations, disappointment and grief.

If that’s not enough, the trauma of tragedy and the destructive forces of disaster are never far away. Even when things go well, prosperity can be its own kind of problem.

Consider the sorts of things that tend to crush us:

- A sense of failure
- Loneliness and isolation
- Dreams that don’t come true
- Relationships that don’t work out
- Worry over what we have or what we don’t

Certainly of all the men in the Bible, Job faced as much calamity as anyone and he faced it with more class and Christian character than most people would. Bible scholars believe Job lived in a remote area where the common religious practice was worship of the stars and planets known as Sabianism. Yet, in the middle of this pagan culture, faced with the most depressing of circumstances, Job found hope in the presence of his Redeemer.

Job 19:25 (ASV) "But as for me, I know that my Redeemer lives, and that he will stand upon the earth at last."

It doesn't matter if Humpty was pushed or not. It doesn't even matter that all the King's horses and all the King's men couldn't help. There's hope for Humpty, and for each of us, simply because we have a King who came!

My fault, your fault, or nobody's fault, God is God, God is good and God is with us. That's why there's Hope for Humpty.

MARY HAD A LITTLE LAMB

Ok, so I know I've already mentioned one nursery rhyme, but here's another one for you. Did you ever consider the ironic significance of the opening stanza of the poem, "Mary Had a Little Lamb"? Originally published in May of 1830, the poem was written by Sarah Hale and supposedly inspired by an actual incident.

Mary had a little lamb;

Its fleece was white as snow.

Everywhere that Mary went,

That lamb was sure to go.

Before the existence of this nifty nursery rhyme, a similar story was played out in Bethlehem of Judea. Mary, the mother of Jesus, gave birth to a son whom John rightly referred to as "the Lamb of God, who takes away the sin of the world!" (John 1:29)

Luke 2:7 "And she gave birth to her firstborn son and wrapped him in swaddling cloths and laid him in a manger, because there was no place for them in the inn."

With a unique combination of prophetic and poetic irony Jesus, "the Lamb of God," was born in a stable. Presumably, there would have been random livestock, including lambs, in attendance for this miraculous moment. In yet another ironic twist, the first visitors to see the world's newborn blessing were shepherds who had been watching – yep, you guessed it, sheep!

Luke 2:8-12, 15-17 "And in the same region there were shepherds out in the field, keeping watch over their flock by night. And an angel of the Lord appeared to them, and the glory of the Lord shone around them, and they were filled with great fear. And the angel said to them, 'Fear not, for behold, I bring you good news of great joy that will be for all the people. For unto you is born this day in the city of David a Savior, who is Christ the Lord. And this will be a sign for you: you will find a baby wrapped in swaddling cloths and lying in a manger'…When the angels went away from them into heaven, the shepherds said to one another, 'Let us go over to Bethlehem and see this thing that has happened, which the Lord has made known to us.' And they went with haste and found Mary and Joseph, and the baby lying in a manger. And when they saw it, they made known the saying that had been told them concerning this child."

The shepherds left their lambs to see the Lamb and Savior sleeping in a manger. Furthermore, the lambs the shepherds had been watching were raised not only for food, but also to be used for sacrifice at the temple. None of this symbolism would have been lost on the shepherds nor Mary and Joseph. Mary had a little lamb. A lamb who lived and died without one act of selfishness or sinfulness, without guile or gall, without a hint of hate or malice, even though He himself was treated poorly by the very people He came to save.

Not only was this Lamb destined to be our savior, but also He was appropriately named Immanuel. Again notice the poetic / prophetic irony, "And everywhere that Mary went the lamb was sure to go." He's still doing that going-with-us-everywhere thing! In the moments and days that followed the sacrificial death of her first born son, Mary the mother of Jesus would discover the power of His promise to "never leave nor forsake." (Hebrews 13:5) and to be "with you always even to the end of time." (Matt 28:20)

That promise is true for each of us as well, regardless of the day or its difficulty, and regardless of our failures and shortfalls, maybe even because of them. Mary's little Lamb, in all His perfection, persists in loving those of us who would be lost and condemned without Him. Mary had a little Lamb indeed; a spotless, faithful lamb and she named Him Immanuel.

INSEPARABLE

Can anything separate us from the love of God, the God who's with us? This is not a new question. It's the question Paul asked in Romans 8:35a, "Who shall separate us from the love of Christ?"

There are a lot of things that try to separate us from God's love. Although the love of God is "our refuge and strength, a very present help in trouble" (Ps. 46:1), that reality is often difficult to discern.

Paul gives the Romans, and us, a heads up on just how far Jesus, Immanuel, would go to bridge the gap that the Fall created. But first he gives a brief exposition on what would work to separate us in the form of another question.

Romans 8:35b (NIV) "Shall trouble or hardship or persecution or famine or nakedness or danger or sword?"

That's a pretty impressive, although short, list. It isn't a list of inconveniences or trivial discomforts! This is a list of real problems that threaten life and living. Furthermore, Paul wasn't talking theory or religious smack. He asked from an experienced perspective.

2 Corinthians 4:8-9 "We are afflicted in every way, but not crushed; perplexed, but not driven to despair; persecuted, but not forsaken; struck down, but not destroyed;"

Truthfully, there's much in this life that would seek to rob us of the awareness or the realization of God's love for us. Maybe today has been one of those days when something has caused you to feel far from the love of God. (The key word in that last sentence is "feel.")

God's love for us is a never-changing reality! Believing that is the highest priority of our faith! Back to the original question: Can anything separate us from the love of God, the God who's with us?

Romans 8:37 (NIV) "No, in all these things we are more than conquerors through him who loved us. For I am convinced that neither death nor life, neither angels nor demons, neither the present nor the future, nor any powers, neither height nor depth, nor anything else in all creation, will be able to separate us from the love of God that is in Christ Jesus our Lord."

Immanuel, GOD with us. All day, every day, and nothing is gonna change that!

WHO IS HE?

Jesus asked the disciples in Matthew 16:15, "But who do you say that I am?"

We've spent the first 11 days of the countdown considering a list of different truths about the God who's with us. I'd like to be a bit more specific these next several days. We'll work our way through several descriptions that lend revelation to our limited understanding. The more we know and believe about who He is, the more we can know and believe about who we're made to be.

Revelation about His nature and character will disarm the devil and empower our faith!

Today's descriptive of God's character comes from John 14:6 when Jesus described Himself as the Way.

John 14:6 "Jesus said to him, 'I am the way, and the truth, and the life. No one comes to the Father except through me.'"

Jesus is consistently making a way where there seems to be no way. You could even say He's the way-maker.

When I was in the military, I went through Jungle Warfare School in Panama. The part of Central America that we were in is thick with triple canopy jungle, populated with jaguars, caimen, (a type of crocodile), and killer bees. Yes, I did say killer bees. Of course, the biggest challenge was just the jungle. It's thick action. Navigating was difficult and done with map, compass, and machete. Picking the right path through the madness was as important as the persistence and patience necessary to work our way through the undergrowth. There were times when it seemed we would never get through, only to find that just beyond the thickest vegetation was the clearing we were looking for.

When we consider this life and all that it holds, we can safely say that it's a jungle out there! That's not to say it's all negative; and in fact, the jungle is simultaneously beautiful and dangerous. Navigating this dichotomy is more than we can do alone. We need a jungle guide, someone who has been there before, and who won't abandon us when the darkness closes in. That's what we have in Immanuel!

Hebrews 4:15 (The Message) "We don't have a priest who is out of touch with our reality. He's been through weakness and testing, experienced it all"

Hebrews 13:5 "I will never leave you nor forsake you."

John 8:12 "I am the light of the world…"

Of course, Jesus is not only a way-maker, but He is the way. That's good news because there are times when we just don't know which way to go, what to do, or where to start. If you don't know which way to go, go toward Him, follow Him, hold on to Him.

What are you navigating today? Have you been trying to go it alone? If so, how's that working out for you?

Maybe you're thinking you only need Immanuel when life gets tough. I will admit that some things seem to require a little more of His eternal input, like praying for a paralytic. But be advised, every day requires its own kind of divine intervention. Being who God made us to be in this world isn't possible without God. There's just "no way" to live the God-life without God.

WHO IS HE? He is the way, and He's the way-maker too!

OUR GREAT GOD

Psalms 95:3 (NLT) "For the LORD is a great God, the great King above all gods. He owns the depths of the earth, and even the mightiest mountains are his. The sea belongs to him, for he made it. His hands formed the dry land, too. Come, let us worship and bow down. Let us kneel before the LORD our maker, for he is our God. We are the people he watches over, the sheep under his care."

Psalm 147:4-5 (WEB) "He counts the number of the stars; he calls them all by name. Great is our Lord, and mighty in power; His understanding is infinite."

I love the Psalmist's reflection on the greatness of God and its evidence in creation! He's not alone in his assessment, check out what Paul said, and then Isaiah after him.

Romans 1:19-20 "For what can be known about God is plain to them, because God has shown it to them. For his invisible attributes, namely, his eternal power and divine nature, have been clearly perceived, ever since the creation of the world, in the things that have been made. So they are without excuse."

Isaiah 40:26 (NIV) "Lift up your eyes and look to the heavens: Who created all these? He who brings out the starry host one by one, and calls them each by name. Because of His great power and mighty strength not one of them is missing."

Did you consider the greatness of God today? He's enough for whatever you've encountered or will encounter. He's not small or incapable!

This is not an attempt at creating a worship moment, though worship is an appropriate response to such a reminder, but rather an effort made at empowering faith for everything that is the God life.

Let me say it this way: the understanding you have of God determines everything else you believe. It determines your relationship with Him, it determines the way you live, and it determines the way you communicate Him to others.

So let me ask it again, did you consider the greatness of God today?

Consider the prophetic announcement that preceded His arrival, and how He even chose His own name!

The name, Immanuel, announced in Matthew 1:23, was first given to Jesus by the prophet Isaiah 700 years before His birth.

Isaiah 7:14 (NIV) “Therefore the Lord himself will give you a sign: The virgin will conceive and give birth to a son, and will call him Immanuel.”

That's impressive! That's God! That's Immanuel, God with us!

TRANSCENDENT

Consider these words from some of my favorite thinkers:

How big is your God? How big is your universe? Light travels at 186,000 miles (299,792 km.) per second. At that speed, Pluto is 5 ½ hours away, the nearest star 4 years, the nearest galaxy 2 million years.

Keep traveling for 11 billion light years. Look at over 10 billion trillion stars and you would only be at the edge of the universe as we know it, and He made it all!

And God is everywhere! Am I personally present in both my hand and my foot, two places at once? God is personally present in all the cosmos and beyond it.

- Christopher Gornold Smith

Reason's last step is the recognition that there are an infinite number of things which are beyond it.

– Blaise Pascal (Pensées, 1670)

A man can no more diminish God's glory by refusing to worship him than a lunatic can put out the sun by scribbling the word 'darkness' on the walls of his cell.

- C.S. Lewis

In the Book of Job, Chapter 26:11, the patriarch tries his utmost to describe the greatness of God, and then he says, "Behold, these are but the outskirts of his ways, and how small a whisper do we hear of him! But the thunder of his power who can understand?"

This is the transcendence of God, but there is another side of the coin. If God is everywhere, then God is here! He is not distant. Our Immanuel may have come as a baby in a manger, but He's not small.

Acts 17:27-28 "He is not far from each one of us, for in Him we live and move and have our being."

Colossians 1:17 "In Him all things hold together."

Why is this good news? Because only a God so big could care about the things that are so small. Immanuel, (Big God) with us.

OCTOBER

IMMINENT

Today we are considering the imminence/nearness of God.

I was recently asked the question, "If God is truly our Immanuel, 'with us' then why do we speak in terms of his distance from us? Why do we beckon Him to 'come closer', 'draw near', or long for His presence, as if we can escape from it, as if we are so great we can live outside of God? Can we even exist outside of His presence?"

As the commenter and the Psalmist both assert, it's not possible to live outside of His presence.

Psalms 139:1-10 "Where can I go from Your Spirit? Or where can I flee from Your presence? If I ascend to heaven, You are there; If I make my bed in Sheol, behold, You are there. If I take the wings of the dawn, If I dwell in the remotest part of the sea, Even there Your hand will lead me, And Your right hand will lay hold of me."

As I mentioned yesterday, if God is everywhere, then God is here! He is not distant. This is the imminence of God.

Psalm 73:23 (NASV) "But as for me, the nearness of God is my good; I have made the Lord GOD my refuge..."

Colossians 1:17 "In Him all things hold together."

God is a God of detail. Nothing is too little for him. His design is perfect down to the unimaginably small. The building blocks of life: DNA, enzymes, amino acids. The building blocks of matter: atoms, nucleus, protons, neutrons, leptons, quarks.

God knows every detail of my life. Jesus said, "Are not five sparrows sold for two copper coins? And not one of them is forgotten before God. But the very hairs of your head are all numbered. Do not fear therefore; you are of more value than many sparrows." (Luke 12:6-7)

Speaking of sparrows, I did a bit of research about how many sparrows there are in the world. Do you know what I found out? Nobody knows! Nobody takes care of sparrows like God. Nobody keeps up with how many are born, or how many die; nobody but God, of course.

There are over 85 different species of sparrows all over the world. The red-billed sparrow of East Africa congregates in flocks of 20 million. Yet God knows when one dies. I'm not sure that up in heaven there is an obituary for sparrows, but He knows. He's not one to let something even as small as that slip by His notice.

I now know the answer to that old question, -- "If a tree falls in the forest and no one is around, does it make any sound?" The answer is yes. God hears it!

Matthew 10:30-31 (NIV) "And even the very hairs on your head are all numbered. So don't be afraid; you are worth more than many sparrows."

Psalm 8:3-4 (NIV) "When I consider Your heavens, the work of Your fingers, the moon and the stars, which You have ordained, What is man that You are mindful of him, and the son of man that You visit him?"

We cannot be out of His reach, He is with us always.

POWERFUL COMPASSION

Job 11:7 (NKJV) "Can you search out the deep things of God? Can you find out the limits of the Almighty?"

Almighty, as defined by Webster's dictionary, means having complete power, as God.

He created all things and holds all things together, in heaven and on earth. He created the things we can see and even the things we can't, according to what Paul wrote in Colossians 1:16. To take it a step further, consider that our Almighty, Sovereign God has unlimited or infinite power. That means He is capable of doing whatever He wills.

Psalm 115:3 (NASB) "But our God is in the heavens; He does whatever He pleases."

That could be a little disconcerting. I can do whatever I want to a bug because I have more power than it, but that isn't necessarily good news for the bug.

But here's the truth about God and His sovereignty: as much as He is unlimited in power, He's also limitless and perfect in His compassion for us! In fact, He wills to make His love known to mankind. He's perfect in both Compassion and Power.

Deuteronomy 7:8 (NIV) "But it was because the LORD loved you and kept the oath he swore to your forefathers that he brought you out with a mighty hand and redeemed you from the land of slavery, from the power of Pharaoh king of Egypt."

Ephesians 3:17b-19 "that you, being rooted and grounded in love, may have strength to comprehend with all the saints what is the breadth and length and height and depth, and to know the love of Christ that surpasses knowledge, that you may be filled with all the fullness of God...."

In fact, Paul tells the Ephesians that God is literally "rich in love toward us." Immanuel, God who is with us, has chosen to use the power He has over us to love us, on this side of eternity and into the next…(FYI, I'm nice to bugs.)

IMMANUEL IS MERCIFUL

There are few words that describe the heart of our Savior better than merciful! The power of His love and compassion expresses or manifests itself in the form of mercy!

Mercy can be defined as a compassion or forbearance shown especially to an offender or to one subject to one's power. It's also defined as lenient or compassionate treatment.

If you've ever made a mistake that caused someone else a problem or heartache, and all of us have, then you've needed mercy. None have suffered offense more than God, and yet, He's the most merciful!

Romans 5:8 "But God shows his love for us in that while we were still sinners, Christ died for us."

Let's be real, it's not a matter of if, but when we will fail to live what we believe. When we don't do what we could or should, that's when we need mercy.

I relate well with Paul, who in his letter to the Romans expressed frustration with his failure and thanks to God for his subsequent forgiveness and deliverance.

Romans 7:21-25: (NIV) "So I find this law at work: Although I want to do good, evil is right there with me. For in my inner being I delight in God's law; but I see another law at work in me, waging war against the law of my mind and making me a prisoner of the law of sin at work within me. What a wretched man I am! Who will rescue me from this body that is subject to death? Thanks be to God, who delivers me through Jesus Christ our Lord!"

Thanks be to God, indeed! He loves us just the way we are but too much to leave us that way. Immanuel is merciful, and He is with us.

Hebrews 4:16 "Let us then with confidence draw near to the throne of grace, that we may receive mercy and find grace to help in time of need."

IMMANUEL IS THE GRACE WE NEED

Ephesians 2:8-9 (NIV) "For by grace you have been saved through faith, and that not of yourselves; it is the gift of God, not of works, lest anyone should boast."

What do we need when we come to the end of ourselves? What do we need when our best intentions leave us unable to live what we say we believe, when our human effort is exposed as futility and we seem incapable of truly hearing from God, let alone following Him?

The answer is, grace. Any attempt at living a God-life without grace will always lead to frustration and ultimately prove futile. To admit that isn't to admit defeat, but rather to assure victory. Granted it's a victory for which He deserves all the credit. To think anything else would be unwise and prideful, and it would lead to further separation from the power that makes His will walk-able.

Matthew 5:3 CEV "God blesses those people who depend only on him. They belong to the kingdom of heaven!"

James 4:6 "But he gives more grace. Therefore it says, 'God opposes the proud, but gives grace to the humble.'"

Grace isn't something we earn because we please God, nor do we experience it simply because of God's favor, it IS God's favor! Grace isn't a reward for being humble, but a humble response is required to receive grace! To quote an old colloquialism, "Humility is our standing under the spout where the grace comes out."

That "spout" is a close relationship and attentive walk with Jesus. Grace is our position in and with Christ that releases the destiny God has prepared for us. Everything we need to live this life we find in relationship with Jesus; that's grace.

2 Peter 1:3 (NLT) "As we know Jesus better, his divine power gives us everything we need for living a godly life. He has called us to receive his own glory and goodness!"

It's when we allow distance to develop between Jesus and ourselves that we have difficulty accessing His strength for our journey. The trap is in our dependence on our own effort. That effort, even when well intentioned, will short-circuit our dependence on His provision.

Immanuel came to be God with us, not God watching us. He wants and wills to be engaged in our everyday lives and activities as a close friend and faithful guide. We are not made to live outside of that relationship. There aren't words to describe how encompassing, important, and impactful that relationship is to our lives and destinies.

We need Jesus more than a fish needs water. We need Him to be God all day, every day and in everything. That's who He is, and that's why He came- to be close, to be grace, to be God with us.

PATIENCE

Romans 12:12 "Rejoice in hope, be patient in tribulation, be constant in prayer."

Paul gives some challenging instruction to the Romans in this passage; in fact the entire 12th chapter is a serious challenge. Consider verses 14-18: "Bless those who persecute you; bless and do not curse them. Rejoice with those who rejoice, weep with those who weep. Live in harmony with one another. Do not be haughty, but associate with the lowly. Never be wise in your own sight. Repay no one evil for evil, but give thought to do what is honorable in the sight of all. If possible, so far as it depends on you, live peaceably with all."

The rough Ron paraphrase is: bless don't curse, empathize with everyone and in all things, choose harmony and humility, never giving what you get unless it's good, and choose to live in peace and be at peace. That sounds just like Immanuel, and it sounds like something we can only do when we do what we do with Him. He came to love and live among the very people who would take His life, choosing to forgive rather than fight in the face of undeniable hate and unfairness.

Yet the most challenging statement of Romans 12 may well be the one made right in the middle of verse 12: "Be patient in tribulation." Can the words patient and tribulation actually go together?

Tribulation can be defined as a state of great trouble or suffering. Anyone who has lived a minute has experienced a fair share of tribulation, some more than others! One of the hardest things to hear during those times is "be patient". Trouble is one thing we wish we could hurry out of our lives. In fact, pain and patience seem almost incompatible. Yet check out what James the brother of Jesus said in James 1: 2-4: "Count it all joy, my brothers, when you meet trials of various kinds, for you know that the testing of your faith produces steadfastness. And let steadfastness have its full effect, that you may be perfect and complete, lacking in nothing."

The word steadfastness James uses here literally means patient endurance. The joy we count isn't because we like to have "various trials" but rather because of what we learn from them. If we were capable of control, we would navigate our lives around or even away from trouble, but that's just not possible in this fallen world. Original sin is the cause, and Jesus is the solution. When we try to hurry our way through hurt instead of patiently processing it with Him, we actually delay the very help or healing we are waiting for.

None of us like to hear the word wait, and we certainly don't want to wait alone. The big news in this narrative is that we don't have to. Immanuel waits and works with us, giving us the grace to find peace when things aren't peaceful, hope when things aren't hopeful, and patience when our hearts want to hurry. Trusting in Him, pushing into His presence, living in His shadow is the only way we can hope to "be patient in tribulation."

THE GOD OF RESTORATION

I love going to wrecking yards with my father-in-law, especially those with older cars lying around. He's an antique car buff and owns a '37 Chevy 4-door sedan and a '58 Bel-Air. Awesome, right?

He's not wealthy so he hasn't been able to buy them in mint condition or restored, but restoration is part of what he loves anyway. He doesn't take them to shows, he just gets them as close to original as possible, maintains them and occasionally drives them.

I love how he appreciates the original design and destiny of these classics. He, like other classic car guys, sees what the rest of us would call a junker and sees a jewel. It may be in a cow pasture with a tree growing through the hood, but that doesn't deter the true treasure hunter.

As optimistic as these guys are though, some projects are even beyond their redemptive capacities. But that's never true for Jesus. He came to redeem and restore everything and everyone. He walks through the most difficult and desolate places to give beauty for ashes. Where once was only fault and failure, He brings forgiveness. Where once was only bondage and baggage, He restores freedom.

What is in your heart or life that needs restoration today? What seems so far gone that it could never be healed or made whole?

Trust in Immanuel to resurrect, to redeem, and to RESTORE!

Psalms 80:1-3 "Give ear, O Shepherd of Israel, you who lead Joseph like a flock. You who are enthroned upon the cherubim, shine forth. Before Ephraim and Benjamin and Manasseh, stir up your might and come to save us! Restore us, O God; let your face shine, that we may be saved!"

Immanuel, the God of eternal restoration!

THE FREEDOM FIGHTER

Immanuel, the Freedom Fighter! I find myself appreciating freedom and the God who won it for me today.

Galatians 5:1 "For freedom Christ has set us free. Stand firm, therefore, and do not submit again to a yoke of slavery."

Freedom is not me doing whatever I want. When that happens, I'm not free.

That kind of so-called freedom is actually self-rule which equates to an Idiocracy. That's just a different kind of bondage, me being controlled by the evil triumvirate, the unholy trinity: me, myself, and "I". (Yes, I made up the word "Idiocracy." It's a combo word: Idiot + democracy, where only "I" get a vote.)

But, God intended for us to be free!

Free to be His, free to be holy, free to have peace, joy, purpose, passion…

He set us free so we could live and walk in freedom.

We were designed for that kind of freedom! Skis are for skiing, planes are for flying, boats are for boating, etc…

Yet we could never attain nor maintain the freedom we were made for.

Paul points this out with impact in his letter to the Romans in Chapter 7, verses 18-21, 24-25: "For I know that nothing good dwells in me, that is, in my flesh; for the willing is present in me, but the doing of the good is not. For the good that I want, I do not do, but I practice the very evil that I do not want. But if I am doing the very thing I do not want, I am no longer the one doing it, but sin which dwells in me. I find then the principle that evil is present in me, the one who wants to do good…Wretched man that I am! Who will set me free from the body of this death? Thanks be to God through Jesus Christ our Lord!"

Thanks be to God! Thanks be to our Immanuel.

LOVE IS STRONG MEDICINE

1 John 3:16 (NLT) "We know what real love is because Jesus gave up his life for us."

Thinking about my dad today; it's his birthday. He was born in 1938 and joined Jesus in eternity in 2007. I'm thankful for the life and love we shared while he was here, and I'm even more thankful for the love and life Jesus gave so he could be there!

Dad wasn't involved in church or in any way vocal about his faith when I was a kid. I think he let the looks and condemnation of others keep him away from the God life he was meant to live. He was a good dad, but not the spiritual leader of our home he could have been. His dad had had his own battles with belief and only came to Jesus at the last moments of his life. In fact, Grandpa Barnard left when Dad was only 11 years old.

We certainly didn't lack for Godly family or even fathers who were involved in church and the things of God. My grandpa on Mom's side pastored the church in which I grew up, and there were always men of God, even uncles, who set an example of what faith and family could look like.

Still Dad was the most important and safest place for me to grow and learn, even about God. He backed Mom up anywhere he needed to about our being in church and following God. More importantly he was my friend. Having a dad believe in and want to spend time with me spoke to me about the love our eternal Father has for us. Love is strong medicine.

Also, he kept me busy and out of trouble, a very important and demanding job for sure. We did a lot of outdoors things together like camping, fishing, hunting and the like. We always had a big garden, some sort of livestock (even if it was only a cow or two) and anytime he was working on something outside, my brother and I were working on it with him.

Unfortunately, we found out in his fifties that Dad was suffering from chronic obstructive pulmonary disease. We knew he was struggling but didn't know why. The 30+ years of smoking took a toll and he paid a high price physically, especially in the last few years of his life. The lack of health in his late 50s until his death just before his 70th birthday, kept him from doing many of things he had enjoyed before his illness. He even had to have a supplemental oxygen source to aid his struggling lungs. My brother kept his tiller and tractor operating for him so he still gardened for as long as possible, but the other outdoor activities were greatly reduced or stopped all together.

Ironically, one thing that never decreased, but actually only increased, was his awareness of God's love for him and the attention he paid to it. Love is strong medicine! In the last few years of his life Dad became more engaged with Jesus in every area of his life. During that time, my brother and sister planted a church, called Legacy of Faith. He called Legacy of Faith "his" church, and was as faithful as possible. Immanuel was with my dad right to the end of his journey. In a classic case of redemption, even as his physical health declined, his spirit was being made whole. The unrelenting love of Immanuel is strong medicine indeed! (Happy birthday, Dad, and thanks, Jesus!)

Ephesians 2:4-5 "But God, being rich in mercy, because of the great love with which he loved us, even when we were dead in our trespasses, made us alive together with Christ…"

PERFECTION AND COMPLETION

Our God is a God of perfection and completion. In a pragmatic sense, this is obvious in His use of the number 7 in His Word.

Certainly the number seven is a constant in the natural world. There are 7 continents, 7 days in the week, 7 notes on the musical scale, 7 primary colors, and 7 directions (left, right, up, down, forward, back and center). That's the short list of examples that exist in the created world.

Beginning with creation, the Bible and its historical record are also full of examples of God's use of the number 7 to illustrate His perfection and completeness.

Genesis 2:2 "On the seventh day God finished his work that he had done, and he rested on the seventh day from all his work that he had done."

Every seventh year was a sabbatical year (Leviticus 25:4). Seven times seven reiterates the sense of completeness. In the Year of Jubilee (at the completion of 7 x 7 years = the 50th year), all land was freed and returned to the original owner (Leviticus 25:10).

The command to forgive "seventy times seven" (Matthew 18:22) reiterates this further. The Lord was not giving Peter a mathematical number of times that he should forgive another person, but rather was insisting on limitless forgiveness for a brother's sin.

Maybe the coolest revelation of God's use of the number 7 to illustrate completeness is found in the book of Revelation.

Revelation 10:7 "In the days of the trumpet call to be sounded by the seventh angel, the mystery of God would be fulfilled, just as he announced to his servants the prophets."

Wow, Immanuel rocking with math! From Genesis to Revelation, and in the world He created, God declares His perfection and completeness. Yet nothing is more perfect or complete than Immanuel's love for each of us. Seriously though, His favorite pattern is loving you.

TRUST IS A MUST

I'm writing this devotional while in flight to South Africa. Flying always makes me consider what it means to trust. Here I sit 38,000 ft. above not only sea level, but literally the sea. Lots of people say they believe air travel is safe and that they trust airplanes. However, the trust part of that statement is technically tested when you're high in the sky.

Undoubtedly and unconditionally, I'm counting on this plane and its pilots to transport me and all those with me safely to our destination. We aren't trusting air travel in theory, but rather in practice. The moment we stepped onto this plane that decision was made. You can't just decide to bail out. They won't open the door and that first step would... well, you get my point!

I sometimes wish trusting God was that pragmatic. You're in or out, and no take-backs. But that's not how grace works. Immanuel came so we could come, and keep on coming.

Still, we would reach our destination sooner if we applied a little staying with our trusting.

Ephesians 6:13 "Having done all to do to stand, stand therefore..."

Isaiah 40:31 "But they who wait for the Lord shall renew their strength; they shall mount up with wings like eagles; they shall run and not be weary; they shall walk and not faint."

Proverbs 3:5-6 "Trust in the Lord with all your heart, and do not lean on your own understanding. In all your ways acknowledge him, and he will make straight your paths."

The truth is, living doesn't even leave us the option to avoid the risk or dodge all difficulty. Trouble comes whether we run from it or journey with God to and through it. I like the "with God" plan best for sure. After all, there is no other plan.

HE IS WITH ALL OF US

Driving across Zambia in route to the Village of Hope of western Zambia you get to see views of rugged and beautiful land, and the seven hour trip is full of people. Oh, it's not crowded. In fact, it's generally rural in nature and relatively sparsely populated. That's not how it feels when you're in Lusaka, though. Lusaka is overcrowded and hectic.

The people here are like people everywhere, some are nice and some are not. Some do the best they can with what they have, and others have given up trying.

Some, maybe even most, live in a darkness I can't really describe. Some have met the One True Light, and follow Him to an undeniable freedom, even in the midst of difficulty and poverty.

On one of my trips, the drive revealed the beauty of an African sunset, the wonder of wildlife that still runs free on the plain, and a tree so large that it could be a small apartment building. The drive and the view through the windshield of our rental vehicle revealed the wonder of the Master's creative handiwork. It reminded me of Him and His transcendent presence.

Leviticus 26:11-12 (AMP) "I will set My dwelling in and among you, and My soul shall not despise or reject or separate itself from you. And I will walk in and with and among you and will be your God, and you shall be My people."

But more than all of that, I was reminded of His unfailing love for ALL people- people who many have forgotten, or maybe never even considered Him. But Immanuel hasn't forgotten them! Neither has He forgotten you.

The only thing He's ever forgotten was my, your, and their sins. Because Immanuel is God with ALL of us!

CHRIST AROUND THE CAMPFIRE

Immanuel is God with us. That's a truth that applies everywhere and against any opposition. Thinking about the challenges during trips to the Zambian bush reminds me of that reality. The demonic strongholds are powerful in the bush and the devil is belligerent in his possession and oppression of the people there. Years of living in darkness without a witness of God's love and light has left people superstitious and afraid. Ancestral worship, witchcraft, and idolatry are a part of everyday life in the bush.

Dealing with that kind of darkness is difficult on so many levels, and yet the grace that God gives makes it one of the most joy-filled assignments ever. In actuality, the darkness makes it easier to see and declare the light. We all share in the assignment and calling to declare His goodness, even when it's difficult to do so.

Acts 13:47 "For so the Lord has commanded us, saying, 'I have made you a light for the Gentiles, that you may bring salvation to the ends of the earth.'"

It's no great surprise that the enemy would oppose the gospel and the hope and freedom it brings. It's even less of a surprise that God would go with those who go for Him. That's not just true now, and it's not just true in the African bush. Men and women of faith have always gone, and are still going, to the far reaches of the earth to proclaim the truth of God and the love He has for people. With each story of obedient faith and fervor comes an amazing story of His faithfulness and favor!

Matthew 28:19-20 "Go therefore and make disciples of all nations, baptizing them in the name of the Father and of the Son and of the Holy Spirit, teaching them to observe all that I have commanded you. And behold, I am with you always, to the end of the age."

"With us always" is a powerfully true promise. I've seen Christ around the campfire redeeming and restoring the most unreached people. Demonic opposition didn't stand a chance against the power and presence of Immanuel, God with us.

A WORK IN PROGRESS

Romans 8:31 “If you continue in my word you are truly my disciples and you will know the truth and the truth will make you free.”

Maybe the most significant advantage to having "God with us" is that He is with us! Let’s face it, sometimes the God-journey can be a bit like walking uphill. It's too much for us to live out on our own!

As much as we may feel like giving up at times, we are called to continue. Such a calling comes with the grace needed to carry it out. In fact, it comes with the Grace Giver as our guide and constant companion. That is to say, He Himself is with us. Every step of every day God is with us.

He doesn't ask us to do what He has not done, nor does He ask us to go where He has not gone. He doesn't call us to continue and then send us off on our journey with a good luck pat on the back as our only support.

Rather, He calls us to follow, and in the following we find our footing and walk in His strength.

Something I often like to encourage others with: "The God who called you is able to do what the God who called you called you to do." You might need to read that one aloud to someone to grasp the good truth.

In this case, He's called us to continue, to follow, and He's promised that He is with us.

A LIFE WORTH LIVING!

Ephesians 2:10 "For we are his workmanship, created in Christ Jesus for good works, which God prepared beforehand, that we should walk in them."

Every 60 seconds, I have one minute less to live on this side of eternity. That obvious reality doesn't make me speed up, it causes me to slow down and consider if what I'm spending my life on will last past when it's gone. I want to walk in all the good works God prepared for me. I am also often reminded of what it took for God to create me and get me here.

Some might say my birth was especially miraculous. Mom had a good bit of issues with her first three pregnancies, which included a set of twins. My four older siblings were all born healthy and such, but varicose veins caused mom enough problems during her pregnancies that she was advised to have no more kids. In fact, she had her fallopian tubes cut and tied, (tubal ligation) after my sister, Thelma, was born. Then she got pregnant, and on December 19, 1965 she gave birth to yours truly.

Apparently, I'm a tube jumper. I know I'm blessed to be here. My whole life people have said to me, "God really wanted you here. He must have a plan for your life."

If that's not enough, on June 11, 2006, I was hit by a truck. Yes, you read that right. I had returned to the church I grew up attending to speak at the Sunday morning service. Immediately after church I was hit by a truck. I was a pedestrian so the odds were stacked in the truck's favor. I had several and significant injuries, and initially was given some pretty negative "prognostications". This story will get its own space in another devotional, but suffice it to say, after a helicopter ride to the hospital, much prayer, some great care, and an undeniable Divine intervention, I survived!

The most common comment after such an event is, "God's not finished with you. He must have a plan for your life." FYI, I don't believe God being "finished with us" is a prerequisite for death. Lots of people we've loved have gone to be with Jesus early, and death is to blame, not God's calendar or work schedule. That may be the deliverance plan for some seasoned saints, but not a viable or necessary explanation for the curse of mortality. What I do know is that He de serves the credit for every miraculous intervention, whether on this side of eternity or the next!

Regardless of the theology on that, the reality is I am still here, and so are you. We're all a miracle, and every day is a gift we've been given. Not just me, all of us.

As long as this fragile and crazy thing called life lasts, I want to make it count. I want to love with a reckless and extravagant love, and I want to love as many as possible for His glory. I want to make His grace and mercy known in this world, to reveal and display His freedom and joy to the bound and burdened. I want to live and tell Redemption's story; I want to make Immanuel known and I know there is grace for me to do that.

Immanuel, God with us, is Immanuel, God through us. I'm using my days to let Him live through me. That's a life we've been gifted to live, and that's a life worth living.

A LIGHT THAT SHINES IN DARKNESS

Here's a simple principle for consideration: light in equals light through.

Isaiah 9:2 "The people who walked in darkness have seen a great light; those who dwelt in a land of deep darkness, on them has light shone."

That's a light I hope you know, and if you do, it's a light I hope you show. I'm not sure it's possible to see it and not show it.

2 Corinthians 4:6 "For God, who said, 'Let light shine out of darkness,' has shone in our hearts to give the light of the knowledge of the glory of God in the face of Jesus Christ."

His light can shine through us even when darkness is pervasive-actually, especially when darkness is pervasive: The darker the dark or tougher the situation, the more obvious the light. That's the unique power of grace and partnership.

I experienced that kind of grace on the day I was hit by a truck. Let me give this story a brief recap and pick up where I left off yesterday. On June 11, 2006, just after speaking at the church in which I grew up, I was hit by a truck. We were about to go to lunch with some family and friends. My cousin's four-year-old son, Caleb, was ahead of Karen and me as we were heading across the parking lot. I noticed this and started to run in an attempt to catch up to him before he got to the highway. Unfortunately, I didn't quite make it! Just as I was catching up, Caleb ran directly in front of an oncoming Ford F-150 traveling at 30-45 mph. I left my radar gun at home so I wasn't completely sure, but suffice it to say, he was going faster than me.

I don't remember deciding to run after Caleb, and as heroic as it all sounds, the more accurate truth is that I was desperate. In fact, I've never felt so desperate in my entire life. I really thought both Caleb and I were going to die. What I knew was that I couldn't watch him die. By the grace of God and by way of a Holy Spirit kick in the seat of the pants, I chased Caleb in front of the truck and managed to toss him just as the truck hit me. It was so close for Caleb that the side view mirror actually caught a bit of the skin and hair from a scuff it gave him on the side of his head. Otherwise, he did a bit of a combat role and landed on his feet in the driveway across from the church. He's a tough little dude.

It didn't go quite so well for me. I took a solid shot and was knocked about 40 – 50 feet, landing under a tree in the ditch. I had varied significant injuries to include a shattered femur, a crack on the head that caused a concussion and significant bleeding, a contused lung that was causing internal bleeding, and a seriously tweaked spine, all of which were accompanied by various other cracks and bruises.

Karen witnessed all of this from the side of the road and thought for sure I had been killed. I think her trauma was more significant than mine. The driver of the truck was also very freaked out. His name is Tony, and as he told me later, he thought both Caleb and I were dead. He had no chance to swerve to miss us, and didn't even get to the breaks until after impact. He said he closed his eyes and couldn't get them open for a few moments.

I should interject here that Tony was a self-proclaimed atheist. He came to visit me the next week in the hospital, and explained the reason he didn't believe in God was because he had never seen anything miraculous. I told him you have to keep your eyes closed to miss the miraculous. He said what he saw that day was indisputable!

Tony told me he saw at least 5 miracles that day. Miracle # 1, Tony said, was when he finally opened his eyes to see Caleb in the mirror. Caleb was standing in the driveway. Yay, Jesus! Then, he saw me in the ditch. By now Karen had found me and was frantically praying over me. Tony jumped out and ran to her. They both thought I was dead.

Miracle # 2, for Tony, occurred when I wasn't dead and I regained consciousness. (The doctors said that regaining consciousness so quickly after such trauma was very unusual.) I think I startled them when I said, "Don't cry sweetie, I'm gonna be ok." God showed up so strongly in the ditch that day. He was definitely a light to me in that desperate place. My face was stuck in the dirt while my foot was up near my head, and I had a pain that was intense, but I had a grace that was beyond description.

Tony said Miracle # 3 was that not only was I alive and conscious, but I was funny. At first he thought I was in shock. The first responders and then the paramedics, (thank God for them), were say ing I might not make it. They called for a helicopter to take me to the hospital, as they were very concerned about my internal bleeding. But I had peace. I had just spoken in church about how we have no promise of another day, and that if this were my day I would be ok with that. I had shared about how God has dominion over death and does healing on both sides of eternity. As I was lying in the ditch, I knew I heard God say I was going to live. I was making jokes and such to try and put people at ease. Jesus, Immanuel, showed up huge for me, and He showed up huge through me. Make no mistake it was all Jesus. Tony saw that; Tony saw Him!

Miracle # 4 was that people came from everywhere and in Tony's words, "prayed like there was a God who heard their prayers." The light was shining in and through them too. If you're ever going to get hit by a truck, try to do it right after church, across the street from church, and speak about how Jesus has dominion over death. Just a thought.

Finally, Miracle # 5, the coolest of all, Tony said, "Here I was, a self-proclaimed atheist, in the ditch with a guy I just hit with a truck. The paramedics are saying he's probably not gonna make it, and I was sure I myself felt the presence of a God I had never believed in".

Right there in the ditch that day Tony Merrit took a knee and gave his life to Jesus because he could see Immanuel, and He could see that He is God with us.

Matthew 5:14-16 "You are the light of the world. A city set on a hill cannot be hidden. Nor do men light a lamp, put it under the peck-measure, but on the lamp stand; and it gives light to all who are in the house. Let your light shine before men in such a way that they may see your good works, and glorify your Father who is in heaven."

WORTH THE HURT

God with us is powerfully manifested by the way we are with each other. That's true because He works through us! His love has maximum impact when shared through close and connected relationship, but that's risky. In fact, our willingness to live vulnerably is critical to closeness and closeness is often what is necessary for someone else's redemptive miracle.

Colossians 1:27 “To them God willed to make known what are the riches of the glory of this mystery among the Gentiles: which is Christ in you, the hope of glory.”

You might say, "I don’t want to get close to people," but I would say getting close to people is one huge way we live close to God. Walking with Jesus moves us to walk with and care about others. In walking with others we see and experience the love of God. When we choose to play it safe, to keep others at a safe distance, we're also keeping Jesus at arm’s length.

Immanuel isn't God with me, He's God with us. I will never experience a full revelation of His heart for me unless I embrace His heart for others. The life of connectedness and compassion is risky, but it's also very rewarding! The cost is real, but the return is worth it.

I like how Shakespeare put it, “He is not worthy of the honeycomb who shuns the hive because the bees have stings.” The bees do have stings. Not surprisingly, hurting people are hard to help. Dysfunction, addiction, and despair are difficult to push through, but the beauty of deliverance surpasses any price. Clearly, Christ reckoned redemption and relationship worth His own life, which makes it less than surprising that He was quick to show compassion.

Matthew 9:36 “When he saw the crowds, he had compassion for them, because they were harassed and helpless, like sheep without a shepherd.”

His compassion is also our calling. His legacy is our leading. Our heart to help should far outweigh any concern of potential for hurt. After all, He is Immanuel, God with US. Christmas isn't just a time for remembering Jesus, but is a time for remembering others. In fact, that might be the best way to honor Immanuel.

SUSTAINER

The Bible teaches that Jesus sustains the universe and everything in it. That certainly includes each of us! In Colossians 1, Paul affirms that in Christ "all things hold together" (v. 17, NASB). The universe is actually held together by the power of Christ.

George Lightfoot noted that the Lord "impresses upon creation that unity and solidarity which makes it a cosmos instead of a chaos."

In Hebrews 1:3, Paul points out that Christ is continually upholding all things by the word of his power. Paul uses the Greek word, pheron, a present tense participle, to tell us that it is currently happening, real time.

Richard Watson wrote that "the Creator has not so fixed and ascertained the laws of nature, nor so connected the chain of second causes, as to leave the world to itself, but that he still preserves the reins in his own hands."

Simple version, Jesus sustains.

He doesn't determine the choices we make, nor does He keep us from all trouble or harm, but He does sustain us through it!

That's why Paul could praise Him from prison, Daniel could declare His faithfulness from a lion's den, and why we can persist with peace in problems or prosperity.

Immanuel holds us, heals us, and helps us. He sustains.

RUN YOUR RACE

Hebrews 12:1-2 "Therefore, since we are surrounded by so great a cloud of witnesses, let us also lay aside every weight, and sin which clings so closely, and let us run with endurance the race that is set before us, looking to Jesus, the founder and perfecter of our faith, who for the joy that was set before him endured the cross, despising the shame, and is seated at the right hand of the throne of God."

We all have a race to run. Each of us were meant and made to live this life in relationship with God. Immanuel came to us so that none of us would fail to run, nor would we ever have to run alone. We're not all the same, but we all have a graced race to run. I know this truth well. I grew up in a home with a "disabled" sister. Yet in spite of the hurdles she faced, my sister ran her race with awareness that she was the "Joy set before Him". In that revelation, and with eyes on Jesus, she ran to victory!

Mary Jane, or MJB as she liked to say, was born January 12, 1961. Clearly God graced the world and our family with a gift. It didn't take long for my mom to realize that she wasn't quite like other babies her age. She didn't do some things as well or as soon. The doctor reported that she had a condition known as Down syndrome. Down syndrome is a genetic abnormality that causes certain physical and developmental differences from non-Down syndrome folks.

Some of those differences seem to be disadvantageous and we call them disabilities. However, if you knew Mary Jane, you would have realized that she was also very advanced in certain other areas because of her "disability." Things that many of us have to learn seemed to come naturally to her. In fact, she seemed an advanced racerunner in the very things that mattered most.

Jesus said the most important commandments are to "Love the Lord your God with all your heart, and to Love your neighbor as yourself" (Luke 10:27). These she did with excellence and ease. She was the essence of joy, a hug and smile looking for a place to happen. Forgiveness was automatic but hardly necessary since she rarely ever took offense. She chose compassion even when it came with cost and often was needed by the very people who may have treated her poorly.

The very things we often find most difficult to do, the most important things, she did better than anyone I have ever known. She believed in Jesus with an honest and unrelenting faith and fervor. Trusting God was like breathing for her. So you tell me, who is disabled?

Mary Jane went to be with Jesus a few years ago, and the world hasn't been the same since. We're all needed and necessary because we're all His and we all have a race to run. We don't run alone; Immanuel, our God, runs with us. Some just pick up on that a little more easily than others.

Psalms 139:13-16 "For you formed my inward parts; you knitted me together in my mother's womb. I praise you, for I am fearfully and wonderfully made. Wonderful are your works; my soul knows it very well."

SEARCH AND RESCUE

Luke 19:10 (NASB) “For the Son of Man came to seek and to save that which was lost.”

Jesus was, and is, on a mission. Immanuel came to seek and save lost people. He came in search of lost hope, lost or confused hearts, lost dreams and destiny. He came to seek and save.

Psalm 37:39 “The salvation of the righteous is from the Lord; he is their stronghold in the time of trouble.”

Have you ever been in a situation physically where you needed rescuing? We sometimes find ourselves in situations that leave us in need of external intervention. A normal day can become a day marked by difficulty and disaster such that we couldn’t prepare for it even if we saw it coming.

I recently read an article about a couple of hikers who had gotten lost deep in the mountainous forests of Washington State. An unexpected and early winter blizzard had caused them to lose their sense of direction and their way. With no cell signal, the two were in serious jeopardy. Fortunately, the one thing they didn’t lose was hope. The two men were confident that they would be missed and that their friends would know something had gone wrong. They kept doing the things necessary to survive and lived in the hope that someone was looking for them, and that help was on its way. They were right, they were missed and help did come.

Many a man or woman trapped in the rubble and aftermath of an earthquake or storm can tell of the great relief they felt when someone came looking, came listening, for even the faintest cry for help.

Even if you’ve never experienced such a disaster or physical challenge, I’m sure you can relate to a time when life left you feeling lost with no hope of finding your own way out. Know this, you are not abandoned, you are not forgotten. God has come and God can hear. His ears are especially tuned to hear faith’s faintest whisper, even the weakest cry for help.

Psalm 17:6 “I call upon you, for you will answer me, O God; incline your ear to me; hear my words.”

Bottom line: HE CAME, (that's what makes Him Immanuel), to seek and SAVE that which was lost. That's what makes Him GOD with us.

REDEMPTION'S MIRACLE

Psalm 121:1-2 "A Song of Ascents. I lift up my eyes to the hills. From where does my help come? My help comes from the Lord, who made heaven and earth."

Immanuel, the baby in the manger, was a miracle. The work He's done, and is doing, is miraculous. His most amazing miracle must be redemption- the redemption of our sin and souls and the redemption of our situations and pain.

On October 20, 2011, Karen and I were in South Africa. We were on our way to chat with friends about church planting and student ministry. In the early hours of the morning we received word informing us that our friends, Thomas and Angelia, had lost their 8-year-old son, Buck, and Thomas's mom, Ms. Nelma, in a terrible car accident.

Buck was a great little hero for God and a missionary in the making. I'm not sure what his assignment might have been, but I can tell you I was making plans to take him to Africa as soon as he was old enough to go. Nelma was one of the world's all-time sweetest people. She and her husband Tommy had spent a lifetime in mission and ministry and are themselves heroes in the faith!

Yet even this story is not without evidence of God's faithfulness and the power of redemption. Exactly one year after this terrible tragedy, Thomas, Angelia, Karen and I traveled to South Africa together. Being there with them on that day was a testimony to grace beyond comprehension. They were certainly still grieving, and I'm sure always will be. Such loss leaves us with a pain that's never far away, and yet it's not without redemption.

Karen and Angelia spoke at the Devoted to Redemption Women's Conference. Angelia shared about Buck, the love she has for him, and the confidence she has that she will see him again someday. Later that day we delivered some of Buck's toys to two different homes for at risk or orphaned children. To finish off our day, Thomas and Angelia cast vision to church leaders for ministry to people with disabilities with passion and effectiveness.

They did all of this on the one-year anniversary of the tragedy that took their son's life. How? Why? Because redemption is real, and God is with us.

THE RIGHT KIND OF RELIGION

James 1:27 (NIV) “Religion that God our Father accepts as pure and faultless is this: to look after orphans and widows in their distress and to keep oneself from being polluted by the world.”

Overlooked is one thing you’ll never be by Immanuel. He came so we could be included, all of us. His heart for us is the heart we are meant to have for others.

If ever we were meant to do anything “religiously” it was to care about those who are orphaned or widowed. Who are the widows and orphans in your world? They not only exist around the world, they exist in your world.

Every church and community has people who have lost a spouse or who are minus a mom or dad, or both. Find a way this holiday season to reach out to the “distressed,” and watch your own stress level decrease. It’s amazing what walking with Immanuel can do for our hearts and our holiday cheer!

Besides it’s what we “religious” people do. After all, if it weren't for Him we would all be separated from the Father.

Here's a promise Immanuel died to keep: “I will not leave you as orphans; I will come to you.” (John 14:18)

WALKING WITH IMMANUEL

Jesus said in John 8:31-32, (NASB) "If you continue in my word, you are truly my followers, and you will know the truth, and the truth will make you free."

This wasn't just a challenge to be a student of the written Word, but rather a challenge to continue to walk in the truth Christ communicated. That truth would later be recorded by His disciples and gifted to the church as a life-giving, God-breathed blessing.

However, that wasn't the complete fulfillment of John 8:31-32 either. For as John would also write:

"In the beginning was the Word, and the Word was with God, and the Word was God. He was in the beginning with God; and all things were made through Him and apart from Him nothing was made which was made... And the Word became flesh and dwelt among us, and we beheld His glory, glory as of the only begotten of the Father, full of grace and truth" (John 1:1-3,14).

The true message of Christmas is beyond amazing: The second person of the Trinity, the only begotten Son of the Father, the eternal Word, and creator of everything, willed to clothe Himself in our nature and become man, our brother, one of us, with us.

God Himself lies in the manger, completely human, and completely God. But He didn't stop there; He's now with us in a way He wasn't before. The baby Jesus grew into a man who pushed down barriers and broke down walls so He could be with us, so we could walk with Him.

We were the source of the separation; He came to be the solution. FYI, He succeeded in His mission. Don't miss that fact, and don't miss the opportunity today to walk with Immanuel, the living Word. He's the truth that we know (John 14:6). He's God with us!

GOD WITH US

Life is a collection of moments that become days that become years that become a lifetime. With each new moment and day come new experiences. Some are good; some are way more than not so good. In fact, sometimes it can feel as if the world is collapsing around you- just like it did for Chicken Little.

Death is a particularly difficult challenge to face. Our own mortality becomes more real to us the older we get or each time we lose someone we love. Yet we know that even death has no victory over Jesus. Paul says in 1 Corinthians that our mortality will put on immortality. Death shall be swallowed up in victory.

Some might try to comfort with the discomforting statement, "the Lord gives and the Lord takes away," as is written in the book of Job. However, that's a tough statement to ambiguously apply to every situation. What I know about God that always applies here is that He's a giver. He gives grace, He gives hope, He gives peace and joy, and in the face of death, He gives eternal life. I can't think of a greater gift. The enemy is the one who likes to take. His effort to take the life of Christ actually resulted in Jesus gaining victory over defeat and death and thus giving eternal life. Take that! See what I did there…

In this one act, Immanuel joined us in the most challenging part of our life journey, death. Immanuel is with us in facing the grave and is our only hope to overcome it!

Sometimes it can feel like the sky is falling. Helplessness can lead to hopelessness, and depression can overwhelm the strongest heart. Anxiety attacks the core of our confidence in God's love for us and His presence with us. The encouragement He gave Israel through the prophet Isaiah is meant for us as well.

Isaiah 41:10 "Fear not, for I am with you; be not dismayed, for I am your God; I will strengthen you, I will help you, I will uphold you with my righteous right hand.

Courage, not bravery, is God's answer for fear. The hope we have in Him is a hope that doesn't disappoint because it's a hope that sees into eternity.

FYI, we're not Chicken Little, and the sky is not falling. Immanuel is God, and He is with us.

STORM SHELTER

I grew up in the southern United States in Arkansas where severe thunderstorms and tornados are common. In fact, it wasn't unusual for our family and neighbors to head to a local storm shelter when the skies grew dark and the clouds were ominous.

I remember one exceptionally stormy December. Tornados and thunderstorms have usually given way to ice and snow by then but this particular year fall was refusing to segue to winter. It's when cool air clashes with warm air that the most violent storms occur. We literally spent Christmas Eve at the community storm shelter. Between the storms we had come out of the shelter so our parents could evaluate the clouds to see if we would go home and return to our holiday festivities. Two of my sisters and I were sitting on the top of the shelter, (they're sunk into the ground with only the concrete top exposed), chatting about what we expected to get for Christmas the next morning. At that very moment a tornado dropped out of a nearby cloud, forcing us to make a mad dash back inside the shelter.

I remember thinking how glad I was we were still near the safety of our underground sanctuary. If you're caught far from shelter you'll find yourself vulnerable and often in serious danger. Of course even if you find safety, your home and possessions may be damaged or even destroyed. Storms are hectic!

More than once, my life has lived like that Christmas Eve back in 1982. Storms can happen anytime, and often at a time when things are otherwise going well. How can we possibly be safe when things are so unpredictable, when the destructive forces of the Fall are never far away? As David said in Psalms 46:1, "God is our refuge and strength, a very present help in trouble."

We certainly can't afford to wait for the storm to come before we find shelter, and fortunately, we don't have to! Immanuel is always with us. He alone is our only safe place and His eternal provision our only real hope!

Psalms 91:1 (NLT) "Those who live in the shelter of the Most High will find rest in the shadow of the Almighty. This I declare of the LORD: He alone is my refuge, my place of safety;"

BLESSED

Immanuel, God WITH us.

I woke up this morning choosing to be thankful, not because everything is good, but because I'm blessed!

Matthew 5:8 "“Blessed are the pure in heart, for they shall see God.”

Pure in heart isn't something we can pull off on our own! Still, I have to believe that when we choose thankfulness, Immanuel purifies our hearts and our motives and then we can see God.

“Blessed are they who see beautiful things in humble places where other people see nothing.” - Camille Pissarro

I think Camille just described Immanuel, God WITH us.

Blessed not just because I'm blessed, but because Jesus is with me and I am aware.

“Blessed are those who give without remembering. And blessed are those who receive without forgetting.” - Bernard Meltzer

A LIGHT THAT SHINES IN DARKNESS

Isaiah 60:1-2 (NIV) “Arise, shine, for your light has come, and the glory of the Lord rises upon you. See, darkness covers the earth and thick darkness is over the peoples, but the Lord rises upon you and his glory appears over you.”

Isaiah wrote to the children of Israel that "your light has come." He didn't promise the absence of darkness, but he did promise the presence of light. For sure, darkness is an issue; but light is a solution. You don't have to deny the darkness to believe in the light.

Without a doubt the pervasive nature of spiritual darkness is devastating. I wouldn’t dare dismiss that truth, as I have seen it firsthand. Individuals, families, countries, and even continents can be devastated by the unforgiving impact of living without the light of God's love.

But as much as darkness has a negative impact, light is exponentially more powerful and positive! I've seen that first hand as well.

John 1:5 “The light shines in the darkness, and the darkness has not overcome it.”

The first time I went through with Hope Church and the Zambia Project to help plant a church in the bush, we visited the remote village of Nalulau. Western Zambia is rural beyond description, and Nalulau is several hours walk from Mongu, which is itself an impoverished third world city. With no infrastructure, very little to eat, and no safe drinking water, the people here were living under a cloud of hopelessness that I hadn't experienced before. Additionally, the devil was and is working hard to isolate and intimidate by any means possible. Witchcraft and the demonic are prevalent everyday realities. To summarize, it was dark.

On our very first night in the bush we encountered a lady who, though very interested in conversation, wouldn't make eye contact. When asked why, her response was that the witch doctor had put a curse on her and that if she made eye contact with people she would become ill. She also said he had cursed her with barrenness and that she had never been able to become pregnant. Her husband confirmed her story. The guys who were chatting with her simply explained that when we give our lives to Jesus, He breaks the curse of sin and death and every other curse of the enemy. This lady and her husband chose Christ and grace and were immediately saved and set free! In fact, that night around the fireside church service she became the official greeter. When asked why she wasn't getting sick by her fellow villagers, she told them she gave her life to Jesus and He had broken the curse. What an impactful witness! Reminded me of the Samaritan woman at Jacob's well.

Ironically, Nalulau sits next to a beautiful lake. Not a large or clean water source, but good for bathing and for irrigation. The land isn't fertile, but it will certainly grow certain crops. Yet virtually nothing was being grown. After a few days of sharing Jesus, the question came up, "Why are there no crops being grown?" The response was that the land was cursed. I'm not sure if there was an actual curse, or if the curse was in believing the land was cursed. Either way it was manifest darkness. We preached and prayed, and God showed up in the prayer. We prayed every curse be broken and that the light of Christ would shine on this people and this place. Many people came to Jesus that week, and a small but very real church was born.

Almost exactly a year later we passed back through Nalulau with a team from Hope Church. We were on our way to another village where we would again be working to plant a church in the bush. When we pulled alongside the lake in Nalulau for a quick hello, what we saw was astounding. First of all, there were crops. Lots of small gardens had popped up. Subsistence farming had seen a revival in Nalulau! Then I asked one of the villagers about the greeter lady and her husband. She told us they were down by the lake working with their three-month-old daughter in tow. YES, I did say three-month-old daughter. Seems they had gotten pregnant one year before, likely while we were there! Speechless, enlightened, amazed!

He is "a Light that Shines in Darkness" and "the darkness cannot overcome Him." The light has come, and is Immanuel, God with us!

GIFT EXCHANGE

I love white elephant gift exchanges. You know, the kind where everyone brings a gift, numbers are drawn, gifts are chosen one by one, unwrapped, traded, taken and retaken. It's good fun. You never know what you're going to end up with. You might bring something good, but get something not so good in return; or you might bring something not so good and end up going home with a treasure. It's a bit of a gamble, but of course, it's just for fun.

Immanuel came to participate in a Christmas exchange program himself. The exchange wasn't so much gift-for-gift, but it was certainly an exchange. He came and gave all that was good for all who were not.

2 Corinthians 5:21 (KJV) “For he hath made him to be sin for us, who knew no sin; that we might be made the righteousness of God in him.”

The initial and most significant exchange was clearly His righteousness for our sin, but it didn't stop there. Even after our initial redemption, His life and love continues to provide exchange opportunities for those who trust in Him.

Every situation and circumstance we face is met with a grace that allows us to trade panic for peace, hurt for healing, and failure for forgiveness. He's there bringing light to our deepest darkness, hope to our most desperate days, asking nothing in return, except that we trust in Him. That's just one more reason I love Christmas and why I love Christ!

Isaiah 61:3 He came “to give them a beautiful headdress instead of ashes, the oil of gladness instead of mourning, the garment of praise instead of a faint spirit; that they may be called oaks of righteousness, the planting of the LORD, that he may be glorified.”

Immanuel is the only one who can offer such an exchange because He Himself is the gift. He is God with us!

A STAR OVER THE STABLE

Can you see and sense God's presence? I know there are moments when He seems far away, and yet we know He's near. Maybe today you need a reminder of His nearness. Look to the heavens, consider the work of His hand.

I qualify as a bit of a stargazer. In fact, when Isaac and Jacob were little, that was one of our favorite activities. We would wait until a moonless night and then head out to some rural location and check out the stars while lying on the hood of our Jeep. In the northern hemisphere we were looking at such well known constellations as the Big Dipper, Orion's Belt, Leo, Virgo, etc.

My travels to Southern Africa these past several years have given me an opportunity to learn the southern sky. My favorite constellation in either hemisphere is the Southern Cross. Like the North Star for those of us living above the equator, the Southern Cross serves as a navigational anchor point for anyone needing to orient themselves directionally in the southern hemisphere.

Once, when in the very dark Zambian bush, I used the Southern Cross as a real-life example of God's consistent unmistakable presence in our lives. I was preaching around a bushfire, fully aware that in this most rural and desolate place people tend to feel forgotten. With that in mind, I was speaking about the faithfulness of God and his ever-present help when we face difficulty. "I will never leave you or forsake you." (Hebrews 13:5)

I asked the people around the fire if they had ever noticed the stars in their sky that form the shape of a cross. To my surprise, they said that they hadn't. David, one of the guys on our team, had given me a really strong laser known as a star pointer. I used it to point out the Southern Cross, to the great pleasure of and with great impact on the crowd gathered around the fire that beautiful starry night! I shared how Jesus died on a cross for us all and how the stars are a constant reminder of that reality.

Psalm 19:1-4 (NLT) "The heavens proclaim the glory of God. The skies display His marvelous craftsmanship. Day after day they continue to speak; night after night they make Him known. They speak without a sound or a word; their voice is silent in the skies; yet their message has gone out to all the earth, and their words to all the world..."

Of course, God has a history of using stars to reveal His presence. After all, it was a star that directed the wise men to the baby Messiah.

Matthew 2:9-10 (KJV) "When they had heard the king, they departed; and, lo, the star, which they saw in the east, went before them, till it came and stood over where the young child was. When they saw the star, they rejoiced with exceeding great joy."

As I told the Zambians that night, anytime you feel alone or life is just too hard, look up and remember that Jesus, Immanuel, is God with us, always with us.

RESTORATION OF RESEMBLANCE

2 Corinthians 5:18 “All this is from God, who through Christ reconciled us to himself and gave us the ministry of reconciliation.”

Immanuel came to reconcile. He came to bridge the gap between the Father and His children, and bridge the gap He did! That reconciliation brings with it the restoration of resemblance. Christ reveals the Father, and we should reveal Christ. The world is in desperate need of Christians who represent, who are like Christ. How different the world would be if our lives were a manifestation of Immanuel, if we were His hands and feet, if when they saw us, they saw Him?

In John 14:9 Jesus said to His disciples, "If you have seen me you have seen the Father." And in Hebrews 1:3 Paul described Jesus as "the radiance of the glory of God and the exact imprint of his nature."

Just as the Son represented the nature of His Father, we are meant to be a reflection of Christ's character and countenance. Though no one's ever going confuse any of us for Jesus, the restoration of resemblance should lead to an effective reflection of His light in our world. John the Baptist understood this as his call and destiny, and so should we.

John 1:6-9 “There was a man sent from God, whose name was John. He came as a witness, to bear witness about the light, that all might believe through him. He was not the light, but came to bear witness about the light. The true light, which gives light to everyone, was coming into the world.”

As that light shines on us, we reflect it to our world. As with a reflection in a mirror, the key to an accurate representation is an unobstructed line of sight between the object being reflected (Christ) and the reflector (us). "The light that shines in darkness" does so when it / He shines in and through each of us.

The closer we are to Immanuel, the more powerful the relationship, complete the restoration, and impactful the resemblance.

FORGOTTEN PEOPLE

Isaiah 56:1 (NIV) “This is what the Lord says: ‘Maintain justice and do what is right, for my salvation is close at hand and my righteousness will soon be revealed.’”

We live in a world where justice is in demand and at a premium. The reality is that many people suffer from injustice and great unfairness. The call of God to His church is to "maintain justice," yet that is not always carried out.

Traveling these past two weeks in Southern Africa has reminded me just how many people live lives of extreme challenge from disability. Here in Africa people with disabilities are often forgotten or overlooked, even by the church.

Take a quick look at your life and into your world today and find the forgotten people. Who needs an outstretched hand? A good conversation? A meal?

God, help us be the "hand of salvation" that is "close at hand" and help us "do what is right," in Jesus name...

Immanuel, God with us.

NOTHING TO FEAR

Today is Halloween here in the States. First celebrated regionally by Irish immigrants in the mid 1800's, this unique and controversial holiday is historically connected to the ancient Celtic festival of Samhain. They believed that on the night before the New Year, which they celebrated on November 1st, the lines between the worlds of the living and the dead could be crossed. Each year on October 31 they celebrated Samhain in an attempt to appease the ghosts of the dead, which they believed returned to earth to cause all sorts of havoc and even damage crops.

If you always thought Halloween was kind of creepy, you were kind of right. Seems like a good time to remember what Paul said in 2 Timothy 1:7 "God has not given us a spirit of fear, but of power and love and a sound mind."

Ironically, Halloween also has a historical connection to the church. In 609 AD, Pope Boniface IV established a yearly commemoration to martyrs known as All Saints Day. The influence of Christianity ultimately spread into Celtic territory and All Saints Day began to be celebrated by many instead of the Celtic festival. The All Saints Day celebration was called All-Hallows from a Middle English word meaning All Saints' Day. The night before it began to be called All-Hallows Eve and, eventually, Halloween. Sheesh…

All of that is a bit much to sort out as you decide what's right for your family. I always feel moved to pray on Halloween. I pray parents are wise, kids are safe, and that God thwarts Satan and all his plans. No doubt there's plenty to be concerned about with this "holiday." I'm certainly not saying it's wrong to trick-or-treat, give away candy, or have a fall festival for the young or the young at heart. Be advised, I enjoy any chance to focus on kids and candy!

However, my favorite thing about this day is that it is only 55 days until Christmas! Jesus coming to earth to save and redeem the world, now that's my kind of holiday! Because He came, we have nothing to fear, not today or any day!

John 14:27 "Peace I leave with you; my peace I give to you. Not as the world gives do I give to you. Let not your hearts be troubled, neither let them be afraid."

NOVEMBER

WITH US, SUSTAINING US

Immanuel, God WITH us.

God IS with us as evidenced by His daily faithfulness. David, in Psalm 54, cries out to God in song. He is being pursued and is under attack. His prayer is simple and profound.

Psalms 54:1 (NIV) "Save me, O God, by your name; vindicate me by your might. Hear my prayer, O God; listen to the words of my mouth."

Maybe you have felt like every attack of the enemy has been pointed at you lately, or at least a fair share! Attacks are real and can be really difficult to understand or endure. They may have a name and a face, but are more often of the spiritual variety that attacks the heart with hurt and heaviness.

Whatever the case, remember the prayer of Psalms 54. With only 54 days until Christmas, we can be assured that Jesus, Immanuel, hears our prayers and will sustain us.

Psalm 54:4 (NIV) "Surely God is my help; the Lord is the one who sustains me."

INCONCEIVABLE!

Ok, I admit it. I love the movie the Princess Bride. Great cast, great story, and great lines. If you haven't seen it, go watch it now!

My favorite line belongs to the character Inigo Montoya who says to his counterpart Vizzini, "You keep using that word, I do not think it means what you think it means." The word Vizzini keeps using is, of course, "inconceivable."

Inconceivable means "not capable of being imagined or grasped mentally; unbelievable."

It may not have perfectly applied to every situation Vizzini, Inigo, and Fezzik were facing, but it certainly applies to the solution Christ is and has provided for us.

Isaiah 53:5-6 (NIV) "But he was pierced for our transgressions, he was crushed for our iniquities; the punishment that brought us peace was upon him, and by his wounds we are healed. We all, like sheep, have gone astray, each of us has turned to his own way; and the Lord has laid on him the iniquity of us all."

Jesus took our pain and punishment as His own. Our disobedience caused Him to suffer and His suffering brought our redemption! Inconceivable!

Because of His willingness to come, we can choose wholeness and healing. Neither our past nor our pain can trap us, no matter how we feel or how things look. He took our punishment. He suffered so we could be free.

Physical healing is our destiny, and for the believer it always comes, sometimes on this side of eternity and sometimes on the next. But, there is a healing that goes beyond the physical, to both the spirit and the soul. He is that healing. There's no solution for the heart but the hand of God!

If we will commit our need to His provision, the process of transformation will work its persistent miracle of grace in our lives. The result is "inconceivable," and totally "Immanuel," God with us!

THE PRICELESS PRESENT

Some people don't like to be reminded that Christmas is coming. I do understand the sources of the resistance. It may come from a heaviness associated with the loss of a loved one. Missing someone can cause a melancholy mood to settle over the holiday season. If that's the case for you, I pray you can celebrate the great times you had even more than you grieve the times you miss. I pray that Christmas becomes for you a reminder of eternity and the endless life we will have with those we love who have gone to be with Jesus before us.

Another source of dread comes from a frustration over the commercialization of Christmas. It can be stressful to think about buying gifts with money you may not have, or the expense of traveling long distances to see family.

My suggestion is to remember what the Lord Himself said about redemption in Isaiah 52:3 (NIV) "For this is what the Lord says, 'You were sold for nothing, and without money you will be redeemed.'"

All the money that's ever been made, all the gold and diamonds that have ever been found, are not enough to pay one man's sin debt. But it's not about money; it's all about the miracle of God's love and the high price Immanuel paid for our redemption.

That's what Christmas is about and that's why I love it!

Immanuel, God with us.

ROCK SOLID

Isaiah 51:1 (NIV) "Listen to me, you who pursue righteousness and who seek the Lord: Look to the rock from which you were cut and to the quarry from which you were hewn."

Immanuel, the "chief cornerstone" as Paul referred to Him, is the "Rock" from which we were cut! He was and is strong and able to endure. He is as David said in Psalms 62:2, "...the Rock that is higher than I."

If that's the quarry we were cut from, what kind of rock are we meant to be? I'm sure we were made to endure. In fact, as we walk with God and as we walk through the fire, we become a rock like our "Rock!"

1 Samuel 2:2 "There is none holy like the Lord; there is none besides you; there is no rock like our God."

Psalm 144:1 "Blessed be the Lord, my rock, who trains my hands for war, and my fingers for battle."

I'm a bit of a rock hound, an amateur gemologist, as it were. My favorite type of rock is metamorphic. Metamorphic rock starts out as one of two types of rock, either sedimentary or igneous. But under great heat and pressure, sedimentary and igneous rocks become transformed and metamorphosed into a very strong and beautiful rock, or even gemstone. Marble and slate are good examples of common-use metamorphic rock.

Then there are diamonds. Diamonds are formed from carbon trapped in the earth's interior and forced to the mantle during volcanic venting. Scientists believe this process takes place 90 miles below the earth's surface where the pressure is immense and temperatures are a consistent 2000 degrees Fahrenheit. Only under such incredible heat and pressure could such a strong and precious gemstone be formed!

Life certainly has a way of turning up the heat and pressure on us as well. The key is to remember who and whose we are, to trust in His ability to be with us and redeem. When we do, even the most difficult situations can bring out a strength and beauty that reveals the character of our Father. After all He is with us, and He's rock solid!

Deuteronomy 31:6 "Be strong and courageous. Do not fear or be in dread of them, for it is the Lord your God who goes with you. He will not leave you or forsake you."

HE SHINES IN DARKNESS

Isaiah wrote to those who were enduring hardship and had no light of their own for the journey. They were left with a choice, trust and rely on God, or walk in darkness.

Isaiah 50:10 (NIV) "Who among you fears the Lord and obeys the word of his servant? Let him one who walks in the dark, who has no light, trust in the name of the Lord and rely on his God."

We're constantly left with the same choice. In fact, that's our choice even when things are going well: trust in God and walk in light or rely on self and walk in darkness.

If you've ever experienced life in the dark, then you know the choice is a simple one. I've done more dumb things in the dark both literally and spiritually than I care to mention. Not only that, but darkness is scary and even downright dangerous. Can you imagine driving on the interstate or a curvy, country road if cars didn't have lights? Yet many of us speed our way through life day after day wondering why we have so many collisions and catastrophes.

I'm not saying we can avoid the dark, but I am saying we can choose light. "The light shines in the darkness, and the darkness has not overcome it" (John 1:5). The darker the dark, the brighter He shines!

Choosing that light, choosing to rely on God, is a no brainer. Of course, the only reason we even have that choice is because He chose to come. He didn't choose to be God, that's just who He is. But what he did choose was to be God with us!

John 8:12 "Jesus said, 'I am the light of the world. Whoever follows me will not walk in darkness but will have light of life.'"

Fifty days until Christmas and here's a not-so-subtle reminder that we don't have to journey alone. Immanuel is "God with us," and He is the light we need and the light we need to choose.

REST

Life can be anything but restful. Our daily pace is often overwhelming. This I know well, I do tired as well as anyone.

In addition to that, the weight of life itself can make rest a seemingly unattainable commodity. Family, work, church, travel, and even a vacation can leave us needing a vacation. The things that rob us of our rest are too many for even a long list. Triumph and tragedy, problems and prosperity all take a toll and come with a cost, and often that cost is rest. Of course, I'm not just talking about physical rest here. Our souls need sanctuary as well.

I'm not suggesting rest is all we need. Certainly, we have work to do. He hasn't called us to the lazy life. He's simply called us to do the work that's worth doing. Working is necessary and rewarding, but working without resting makes work difficult to do, and impossible to do well.

Knowing this, David gave the Israelites a simple and yet profound exhortation in Chronicles 22. They were beginning the overwhelming work of building the temple while facing significant opposition.

1 Chronicles 22:18 (NIV) "He said to them, 'Is not the Lord your God with you? And has he not granted you rest on every side?'"

This simple reminder is a good one for us as well. He's called us to work, and simultaneously given us rest. While getting tired is necessary, staying tired is not! The key to doing both work and rest well is to remember the Lord our God is with us, and He has granted us rest.

IMMANUEL ON THE THRONE

It's that time of year here in the states when elections take place. I'm really thankful we live in a society where we have a voice. I know some of you are in other parts of the world and from political environments where that may not be true for you.

Many would say one vote doesn't matter, to which I would say, "Appreciate what you do have rather than lamenting what you don't." Others would be thankful for the process flawed, as it may be, that we take for granted! I wish a lot of things were different, or better. Then again, I wish I were better at deciding what better is and what should be different. Sorting out what to do and how to vote should humble us and move us to prayer. Then when the elections are done, we must heed the instruction of the Lord to continue to pray for our government and those who lead it.

1 Timothy 2:1-4 "First of all, then, I urge that supplications, prayers, intercessions, and thanksgivings be made for all people, for kings and all who are in high positions, that we may lead a peaceful and quiet life, godly and dignified in every way. This is good, and it is pleasing in the sight of God our Savior, who desires all people to be saved and to come to the knowledge of the truth."

I'm thankful God has honored our imperfect efforts to live and govern fairly and freely. At the end of the day whatever party or candidate you prefer, we are all Americans and grateful to be. But what I'm even more glad about is more cross-cultural and bipartisan. I'm glad that God / Immanuel is with us. Not even, or only, with government, or church, or nation, but specifically and especially with us.

Wherever you live in the world, whether free or oppressed, voter or victim, remember your King is the King of all kings. He, "Immanuel," isn't up for election, but rather He has chosen the church as His elect.

Ephesians 1:22-23 "And he put all things under his feet and gave him as head over all things to the church, which is his body, the fullness of him who fills all in all."

Immanuel is on the throne, and that makes me glad...

ALL IN

He is completely and totally with us. He hasn't held Himself out of any part of our lives, good or bad. He's a God worthy of our complete surrender. Still, we often hold ourselves back from Him. We find ourselves in the kiddie pool of possibilities when His plan for us is to be all in. Ezekiel 47, one of my all-time favorite passages, tells the story of a vision Ezekiel had about a massive river that flowed out of the temple.

Ezekiel 47:1-6 "The man brought me back to the entrance to the temple, and I saw water coming out from under the threshold of the temple toward the east (for the temple faced east). The water was coming down from under the south side of the temple, south of the altar. He then brought me out through the north gate and led me around the outside to the outer gate facing east, and the water was trickling from the south side. As the man went eastward with a measuring line in his hand, he measured off a thousand cubits and then led me through water that was ankle-deep. He measured off another thousand cubits and led me through water that was knee-deep. He measured off another thousand and led me through water that was up to the waist. He measured off another thousand, but now it was a river that I could not cross, because the water had risen and was deep enough to swim in—a river that no one could cross. He asked me, 'Son of man, do you see this?'"

I love that question. "Son of man, do you see this?" Do you see what is possible? Do you see the difference an all-in relationship with Jesus can have on your life, on your heart, your peace, your joy? Have you seen the difference He can make on your relationships at home and work, with family and friends? Have you seen this?

There's so much imagery and symbolism in this vision. A river of life, that flows from the presence of God, which can be experienced at many different levels. First ankle deep, then knee deep, then waist deep, and finally over the head and too wide to see across.

That's the degree to which we should want to be lost in Christ. Completely surrounded by and surrendered to Him! No watching from the bank or stopping short of the main channel, but ALL IN, and fully trusting.

WITH US TO THE VERY LAST DAY

I sometimes feel a bit overwhelmed with a sense of my own mortality. A few years ago, I was in a severe accident that nearly took my life. That event further heightened my awareness that life is fragile and each day a non-guaranteed gift! Most of us have had the proverbial close call that took both our breath and our sense of invincibility away for a moment.

I'm not saying this reality should cause us to live a life of fear and dread. Certainly not! As those who believe in forever and the God who created it and us, we put our confidence in Him and our hope in eternity. That's what enables us to live fully and faithfully, the full length of our lives.

In Isaiah 46, Immanuel speaks directly to that point, with His greatest encouragement being that He will be with us.

Isaiah 46:3-5 "Listen to me, you descendants of Jacob, all the remnant of the people of Israel, you whom I have upheld since your birth, and have carried since you were born. Even to your old age and gray hairs I am he, I am he who will sustain you. I have made you and I will carry you; I will sustain you and I will rescue you."

Ironically, the same Isaiah that God speaks to and through here is the Isaiah that shared more prophetic insight about the coming Messiah than any other Old Testament prophet. In fact, this devotional finds its inspiration in Isaiah 7:14 "Therefore the Lord himself will give you a sign. Behold, the virgin shall conceive and bear a son, and shall call his name Immanuel."

Fortunately, we don't have to live this life without God, nor do we have a God who will fail us when it's hard or we are old. Immanuel is the God who was, who is, and who is to come. Neither age nor even mortality is an issue for Him so it doesn't have to be an issue for us either. The way I figure it, He's got me and this life I'm living covered, all the way to the very last day…

TWO ARE BETTER THAN ONE

God makes Himself known to us, and His relationship to us sets the standard for our relationships with others. God didn't create us to be holy hermits. That's an oxymoron. He made us to walk with Him and each other. Not only was Jesus close to His disciples, but His walking with them built this motley crew into a mighty team.

I certainly enjoy spending time with friends and family. Turns out being with each other can have great worth in the kingdom. We're good together, and have more impact in the kingdom because we're friends! I love the way that works and am glad that God designed the Kingdom in such a relationship-driven way.

Ecclesiastes 4:9 (NIV) "Two are better than one, because they have a good return for their labor."

Ephesians 2:19-22 "So then you are no longer strangers and aliens but you are fellow citizens with the saints and members of the household of God, built on the foundation of the apostles and prophets, Christ Jesus himself being the cornerstone, in whom the whole structure, being joined together, grows into a holy temple in the Lord. In him you also are being built together into a dwelling place for God by the Spirit."

Not only are we more effective in the Kingdom because of relationship, but we are also better in battle because we walk together.

Proverbs 17:17 "A friend loves at all times, and a brother is born for adversity."

Ecclesiastes 4:12 "And though a man might prevail against one who is alone, two will withstand him—a threefold cord is not quickly broken."

Don Everts, in *Jesus with Dirty Feet*, defines the church as "a bunch of kingdom dwellers following Jesus together. (Steeples and pews not included.)"

Find a friend and be a friend today. Life lives better for us and others when we walk it together. The Master's model is together. We really are better together! That's the way Immanuel set things up...

WITH US IN BATTLE

Daniel 3:24-25 "Then King Nebuchadnezzar was astonished and rose up in haste. He declared to his counselors, 'Did we not cast three men bound into the fire?' They answered and said to the king, 'True, O king.' He answered and said, 'But I see four men unbound, walking in the midst of the fire, and they are not hurt; and the appearance of the fourth is like a son of the gods.'"

Immanuel, God with us, came as so much more than a baby in a manger. He came as a faithful friend and deliverer. Jesus bridged the gap between heaven and earth and is with us even now, fighting for us. Though we may feel cut off in battle, in reality we are never alone.

During the Vietnam War at the battle of Khe Sahn, 6,000 marines held out against 40,000 North Vietnamese soldiers because they were constantly re-supplied via air drops. Every day, no matter how difficult their situation, they knew help was on the way. They weren't relieved of their duty, but they were supported and re-supplied from above.

Additionally, there are many World War II stories from people who held onto hope against the terror caused by their Nazi invaders simply because they knew the conquering armies of the allies were on the way.

While in a Nazi prison camp, Betsy Ten Boom was quoted by her sister, Corrie, as having said, "There is no pit so deep that He is not deeper still." That's an amazing proclamation of faith that can only come from a real awareness of His presence.

At times we may feel like we've inherited our own little piece of hell here on earth. It's as if we're being pelted all at once by hell's heaviest arsenal. In the middle of such a calamity, you might feel like saying "I just don't have enough faith to believe God will come through."

We serve a God who is with us in battle. Believing that and trusting Him is a choice, and we have the grace to choose it. God's means of deliverance and help are as varied as the problems and people who face them, but are always delivered by God Himself! We can be confident in our deliverance. Whatever our problem or challenge, we don't face it alone, we don't face it without grace and we don't face it without God. He is with us.

Although I'm certainly amazed at the faith of the three Hebrew boys in Daniel Chapter 3, I think it's safe to say Hananiah, Mishael, and Azariah fully expected to lose their lives for the stand they made. They hoped for a miraculous deliverance, but by their own testimony were prepared to face the fire.

Daniel 3:17-18 "If this be so, our God whom we serve is able to deliver us from the burning fiery furnace, and he will deliver us out of your hand, O king. But if not, be it known to you, O king, that we will not serve your gods or worship the golden image that you have set up."

Know whatever the battle you face today, there is a fourth man in the fire, and He is Immanuel, God with us.

THE POWER OF PARTNERSHIP

Certain statements the Bible makes are impossible for the unaided Christian to carry out. That's true for even the strongest believer or the most disciplined effort.

Matthew 5:48 "Be perfect, therefore, as your heavenly Father is perfect."

1 Peter 1:16 "It is written, be ye holy; for I am holy."

Ephesians 5:20 "Always give thanks to God, the Father, for everything."

Philippians 4:6 "Do not be anxious about anything."

1 Thessalonians 5:17 "Pray without ceasing."

Words and phrases such as "perfect," "holy," "always," "about anything," and "without ceasing," are daunting if not undoable without divine intervention!

"The business of living the Christian life as it should be lived is too lofty in its ideals and too exacting in its demands for us to engage in it alone. We desperately need a partner with adequate capital to make it a success." Oswald Sanders

That partner is Immanuel. He is God enough and His grace is real enough for us to live the life He calls us to live. The key to living the God-life is letting God be God. He's not just our partner, He's our Lord. When we let Him lead, we can succeed.

What would otherwise be impossible becomes our clear and attainable destiny. In fact, it's because of who He is that we can be who He made us to be, and because He is with us that we CAN live the life we were made to live.

Philippians 4:13 "I can do everything through him who gives me strength."

THE POWER OF SURRENDER

We need Immanuel, God with us. We cannot walk with God without God; and we cannot walk with God and continue to go our own way. Not even in the little things, especially not in the little things.

Our part is to surrender control to the senior partner.

James 4:7 (NIV) "Submit yourselves, then, to God. Resist the devil, and he will flee from you."

Romans 12:1 (NKJV) "I beseech you therefore, brethren, by the mercies of God, that you present your bodies a living sacrifice, holy, acceptable to God, which is your reasonable service."

Surrender means to yield ownership, to relinquish control over what we consider ours: our property, our time, and our "rights."

Surrendering to God helps us to let go of whatever has been holding us back from God's best for our lives.

Surrender isn't losing, but rather the only way to spiritual victory.

Adam and Eve had a choice, and although we won't find fruit from the tree of the knowledge of good and evil in the produce section of the local grocery, we too have choices.

Mark 8:34-37 "And calling the crowd to him with his disciples, and said to them, 'If anyone would come after me, let him deny himself and take up his cross and follow me. For whoever would save his life will lose it, but whoever loses his life for my sake and the gospel's will save it. For what does it profit a man to gain the whole world and forfeit his soul? For what can a man give in return for his soul?'"

Here's an anonymous poem about dying to self, which a good friend shared with me a few years back.

When you are forgotten, neglected, or purposely set at naught, and you don't sting or hurt with the oversight, but your heart is happy being counted worthy to suffer for Christ; - That is dying to self.

When your good is evil spoken of, when your wishes are crossed, your advice disregarded, your opinion ridiculed, and you refuse to let anger rise in your heart or even defend yourself, but take it all in patient, loving silence; - That is dying to self.

When you lovingly and patiently bear any disorder, any irregularity, any annoyance; when you can stand face to face with waste, folly, extravagance, spiritual insensibility, and endure it as Jesus did; - That is dying to self.

When you are content with any food, any offering, any raiment, any climate, any society, any solitude, and any interruption by the will of God; - That is dying to self.

When you never care to refer to yourself in conversation or record your own good works or itch after commendation, when you can truly love to be unknown; - That is dying to self.

When you can see your brother prosper and have his needs met, and can honestly rejoice with him in spirit and feel no envy, nor question God, while your own needs are far greater and you are in desperate circumstances; - That is dying to self.

When you can receive correction and reproof from God's appointed messenger, and can humbly submit, inwardly as well as outwardly, finding no rebellion or resentment rising up within your heart; - That is dying to self.

To walk with God and let Him be Immanuel, God with us, we must surrender our own wishes, needs, pride and die to self.

NOT ASLEEP!

Ironically, it's 4:23 am here in South Africa. The house is quiet, but my mind is busy, almost chaotic. Everyone is fast asleep and there's a lot on my mind!

I grew up in a home with one brother and three sisters. At one point, when we were elementary age, we all shared the same room with two beds. The three girls were in one bed and my brother and I in the other, with a small gap between the two.

My brother Darrel, who is four years older than me (I'm the baby), didn't like to be the last one to go to sleep. In fact, none of us did, it was kind of creepy!

He made up a little game where anyone who wasn't asleep could say to everyone else, "Not asleep." and if you were awake you were required to reply back, "Not asleep." My brother also determined that if you refused to reply and you were awake, it was the same as lying. We often made such a fuss that even those who were asleep would soon be saying "Not asleep!" as well!

Worry has a way of catching me in the middle of the night. A simple trip to the toilet can turn into a quiet chaos that makes me feel alone, even if I'm not. Unfortunately, I can't send my brother a 4 am text every time I let anxiety get the best of me, and even my amazing wife needs her beauty sleep. But I do know someone who is ALWAYS there, and who NEVER sleeps! "Hi Jesus, you awake?"

Turns out I'm not the only one who ever fought this battle. The Psalmist wrote a timeless encouragement to us about our Immanuel in Psalms 121, verses 1-4 (NIV) "I lift up my eyes to the mountains, where does my help come from? My help comes from the Lord, the Maker of heaven and earth. He will not let your foot slip, he who watches over you will not slumber; indeed, he who watches over Israel will neither slumber nor sleep."

Then there's what Paul wrote as an anti-anxiety instruction to the Philippians in Philippians 4:6-7 (NIV) "Do not be anxious about anything, but in every situation, by prayer and petition, with thanksgiving, present your requests to God. And the peace of God, which transcends all understanding, will guard your hearts and your minds in Christ Jesus."

I think I'll go back to sleep now, Immanuel's got this covered!

WIDE AWAKE

I wish I were more like Jesus!

In yesterday's devotional I wrote about the "Not Asleep" game my brother invented and how glad I am that God / Immanuel, never sleeps (Psalms 121).

Although we require and definitely need our sleep physically, I think we could stand to be a bit more awake spiritually. As followers of Christ we should be ready to reveal His nature and character at all times and in all things.

"Wide Awake!"

It's easy to fall into the trap of business and distraction and literally sleepwalk through life, but that's not God's will for His children.

Paul, in an outright challenge to the Ephesian church, wrote of our need to be aware, wise and awake.

Ephesians 5:13-16 "But when anything is exposed by the light, it becomes visible, for anything that becomes visible is light. Therefore it says, 'Awake, O sleeper, and arise from the dead, and Christ will shine on you.' Look carefully then how you walk, not as unwise but as wise, making the best use of the time, because the days are evil."

That level of readiness and awareness can only come from a deep and abiding relationship with our Immanuel. When we walk with Him, we're wide -awake! It's then that we can sense and see His hand at work in our lives and in our world. This keeps us safe from deception and makes us effective against the enemy, just like Jesus.

When we walk with Jesus, we walk like Jesus!

John 14:12 (NIV) "Very truly I tell you, whoever believes in me will do the works I have been doing, and they will do even greater things than these, because I am going to the Father."

Not Asleep! Wide Awake!

ON THE GO WITH GOD

For some people the most difficult aspect of ministry in the bush in Zambia is the camping. Honestly, it's easier now than it's ever been. The trucks we rent have amazing tents on top and include a vast array of useful camping gear. Cook stoves, pots and pans, and even a refrigerator are included. The two tents on top of each truck include a mattress, a sleeping bag, a blanket and pillow for four people! It's still challenging though, simply because with all the things to do on the ground, time in the tent is tough to find. But when you get it, you appreciate it.

We find in Exodus that tent time was important for Moses, too.

Exodus 33:7 "Now Moses used to take a tent and pitch it outside the camp some distance away, calling it the 'tent of meeting.' Anyone inquiring of the LORD would go to the tent of meeting outside the camp."

The tent of meeting! I love that phrase! It's very descriptive.

It's used here to describe the Tabernacle of Moses, the place he and the people of God met with God! The Israelites moved a lot, and every time they relocated, the tent of meeting was taken down and set back up at the new location. Moses faced lots of obstacles and opposition as He led the people of Israel in the exodus to freedom. However, he never faced what he faced alone. He would make his way to this famed meeting place, and there He would meet with Immanuel.

We move a lot too! In fact, our lives are lived on the go. Work, family, and even church can keep us so busy that we miss the one meeting we won't do well without. In as much as we are meant to walk with God, we like Moses, still need times in the day when we quiet ourselves before the one who loves us and leads us.

Speaking of terms of description, "with us" describes Immanuel really well too. Thankfully a visit to the modern day "tent of meeting" requires only that we too choose to see and hear, and to be with the God who is always with us.

ASK WITH CONFIDENCE

I love knowing I'm praying the Lord's will! David reaches out to God for help in Psalm 38 in just that kind of prayer. Here, David simply asks God to be who He is. He asks Immanuel to be faithful, to be near, to be on time, to be personal, and to be his Savior!

Psalms 38:21-22 (NIV) "Lord, do not forsake me; do not be far from me, my God. Come quickly to help me, my Lord and my Savior."

That's who He is, that's what He is, and that's what He does. Granted the "on time" part refers to His time not our time, but it will all redeem in time. Honestly, there's so much unique theology about prayer that it can be more complicated than it needs to be. (Unique is code for crazy.) Plus, there's just a lot we will never completely understand about prayer.

But what I do know is that prayer isn't just a petition, it's also a conversation. Prayer isn't where I change God but rather where He changes me. After all, I'm the one who needs changing. I also know that my prayers have a supernatural effect on my heart and the hearts of others. In fact, my prayers have an impact in a realm beyond my present reality in a way that nothing else I do does.

James 5:16 "Therefore, confess your sins to one another and pray for one another, that you may be healed. The prayer of a righteous person has great power as it is working."

Jeremiah 33:3 "Call to me and I will answer you, and will tell you great and hidden things that you have not known."

Maybe you need to say a prayer like the one David prayed; a prayer for His intervention and help. Christmas reminds us of His willingness to come to us and assures of His ability to intervene.

So pray. Pray in faith, and with confidence. Because when we pray we're praying to a God who loves for us to pray, hears us when we pray, and is with us either way.

Jeremiah 29:12 "Then you will call upon me and come and pray to me, and I will hear you."

1 John 5:14-15 (NIV) "This is the confidence we have in approaching God: that if we ask anything according to his will, he hears us. And if we know that he hears us—whatever we ask—we know that we have what we asked of him."

THE GRACE TO LAUGH

Today is our son, Isaac's, birthday. I sure do love that guy! His name really fits him too. Isaac is a Hebrew name and it means laughter. Karen had already miscarried once and struggled profoundly in her pregnancy with Isaac. In fact, he ended up being born at 27 weeks (3 months early). Even though he only weighed in at an underwhelming 1 pound 14 ounces at birth, our baby boy was born with a smile. There wasn't much going well at first, but his heart and his smile have always been strong. Ok, his smile was probably more of a fish face at first, but we knew what he was going for.

It might have been easy for him to smile, though he endured all sorts of pokes and prods, and even lived the first 9 weeks of his life in an incubator. However, it wasn't as easy or natural for mom and dad to smile. We did learn to do so, even in those early and difficult days of uncertainty. In the first moments after his birth Isaac was taken away in a helicopter to a Neonatal ICU, leaving Karen and I praying in a hospital hallway, her still on a gurney. Still, Immanuel was definitely with us.

We've had hard days since then as well, but in them all we've been graced to smile and even laugh. That grace is there even when life isn't living well. Check out the truth recorded in Job 8. Bildad the Shuhite certainly didn't give the greatest encouragement or counsel in most of what he had to say, but he was spot on here:

Job 8:20-21 MSG "There's no way that God will reject a good person... God will let you laugh again; you'll raise the roof with shouts of joy."

We love both our boys. Jacob was also born early and has been an unbelievable blessing. Both he and Isaac have an amazing sense of humor and honor. They cause us to smile with both. I think that's how it is with God as well. We make Him smile with both our honor and our humor. He's the one who inspired the writer of Proverbs 17:22 to declare, "A joyful heart is good medicine."

It's ok to cry too. We've done plenty of that together as well. Even when we do, we usually end up laughing, or at least smiling through our tears. That's all about Immanuel and His being with us. He's the one who has graced us to laugh in the first place.

MASTER CRAFTSMAN

James 1:12 "Blessed is the man who remains steadfast under trial, for when he has stood the test he will receive the crown of life, which God has promised to those who love him."

Immanuel, God with us, is a master craftsman. He builds in a way only God can build. We're His most significant creation, and we are built to last! In fact, He never stops working on or walking with us. That's good news, because life provides a constant challenge to the purposes and plans for which we were made. God on the other hand, is constantly and consistently working His will into our hearts.

We can decide to avoid certain sorts of trouble by choosing to walk in truth and wisdom. But much of what comes our way is simply the result of the Fall, yet we're meant to stand.

Life is full of all sorts of days, and both sunshine and rain, ultimately take their toll. However, with Jesus at work in our lives we will not only survive what happens to us, but also grow stronger because of it.

Choosing to believe that and to believe in Him is key to enduring and remaining steadfast regardless of the day or difficulty it might bring. If our hope is in our own effort or action, we're in big trouble. Only when Immanuel is building the house will the house stand the test of time.

Psalms 127:1 "Unless the LORD builds the house, the builder builds in vain."

The creator is a craftsman. Immanuel is with us, always working on us and in us!

A KNACK FOR NOTICING

Did you ever notice how much we fail to notice?

One of the most amazing things about Jesus / Immanuel is how attentive He is. He simultaneously holds the universe together while keeping an accurate hair count.

Colossians 1:17 “And he is before all things, and in him all things hold together.”

Luke 12:7a “Why, even the hairs of your head are all numbered.”

He noticed a blind beggar by the road, a tax collector up a tree, a sick lady in a crowd, His disciples across the lake in a storm, a woman at a well, a lame man at a pool, etc.

He noticed the not notable, the deeply troubled, and the simply searching. He noticed them all!

The point is He noticed the people and things most of us miss. You might even say Immanuel had and has a knack for noticing.

Then again, that's a big part of what makes Him Immanuel. I guess if He didn't notice He wouldn't be very "with us."

But He does notice, and He has noticed and taken note of you and your situation, and that's one thing we should never fail to notice...

IMMANUEL ON A MISSION

We're meant to live our lives on mission, locally, trans-locally and internationally!

Somehow we seem a bit less motivated and a lot more intimidated with our local mission than with a "missions" trip. It seems the idea that we are missionaries often only applies to cross-cultural ministry.

What about the people in our local context, in our spheres of influence?

Mark 16:15 "And he said to them, 'Go into all the world and proclaim the gospel to the whole creation.'"

"All the world" starts with the world inside and just outside your front door. No one believes in the global mission more than me, and global must include across the ocean! However, global must also include across town, across the street, across the hall, and across the room. These are the places and people to whom we can and should have the strongest and most consistent witness.

Acts 1:8 "But you will receive power when the Holy Spirit has come upon you, and you will be my witnesses in Jerusalem and in all Judea and Samaria, and to the end of the earth." If Santa Claus can make it around the world with gifts, we can make it around the world with the Best Gift. Start in Jerusalem – your immediate community and group of friends. Then Judea – your larger sphere of influence and network. Samaria – a seemingly disliked community. And if, and when, He sends you – to the ends of the earth.

The "all nations" of Matthew 29:18 starts with our nation! Conversely, the same heart that will motivate us to go locally will not allow us to ignore the need to go trans-locally and internationally.

Merry Christmas and welcome to Immanuel's mission. He came to us, and we can GO to them.

SEASON OF THANKSGIVING

This week we are very thankful. We can be thankful for more things and people than we can list.

Thankful for friends and family.

Thankful that God made a provision for death so that we can have hope; not only for ourselves but also for those we love who are here or have gone before us.

Thankful that no matter where we are, He is there.

Thankful that "He works all things together for the good" (Romans 8:28).

Most of all, we can be thankful to God for Jesus, and for His willingness to leave heaven to come to earth to redeem and restore.

I love Thanksgiving, and as much as I love my friends and family here in South Africa and the mission we get to live out together, this is definitely a day I wish I were home.

I love visiting with family and eating turkey, dressing, a little ham, and pecan pie at my mom's house. Watching a little football with my brother and all the guys wouldn't hurt my feelings either.

Still, you don't need to be in America to be thankful. Jacob and I celebrated thanksgiving here in Cape Town with Greg and Angie Pampell and their family, as well as with our new friends the Salemi's. Angie cooked ham and deboned chicken, while Amanda made some awesome snicker doodle cookies.

Even though all of us would like to have been home, we knew we were blessed and were thankful for it.

We even had our lunch attacked by a baboon, which we fought off with a paper plate and a power-aid bottle. I gave him one good shot, but he still got away with a bag of chips. However, we got away with a big laugh, good times, and a new Thanksgiving memory for sure.

Immanuel, God with us. Gracing us, reminding us and causing us to be thankful.

Happy Thanksgiving!

PROMISE KEEPER

The birth of Jesus was the keeping of a prophetic promise made through Isaiah 700 hundred or so years before it's fulfillment.

Isaiah 7:14 “Therefore the Lord himself will give you a sign. Behold, the virgin shall conceive and bear a son, and shall call his name Immanuel.”

I never cease to be amazed at her response to the prophetic revelation that she would become pregnant with the Messiah, "How can this be?" she said. (Luke 1:34) But then her second surrendered saying is even more amazing, “I am the Lord’s servant. May everything you have said about me come true.” (Luke 1:38)

To come to such an attitude of obedient surrender so quickly is amazing, but there was still a long journey, from hearing and believing in the promise to seeing the fulfillment of it.

In Mary's case, not only was there a nine-month pregnancy, there was also the physical distance to be traveled from Nazareth to Bethlehem. The challenge wasn’t so much from point A to point B but rather the journey in between. That's true for us too. The promise was made in Nazareth, and brought to fruition in Bethlehem.

It is about 94 miles from Nazareth to Bethlehem. In Mary’s case that was 94 big time pregnant, donkey-riding miles. What a journey. Can you imagine? Poor Joseph! Ok, poor Mary too. They had to go from Nazareth to Bethlehem to see the fulfillment of God’s incredible promise.

How far are you willing to go?

Many of us can find first faith, but follow through faith seems to allude us. It's often the journey that gets us. More of the Jews died in the wilderness on their way to the Promised Land, than in all the battles after they entered the Promised Land.

The fulfillment of the promise through Mary required her simple faith and complete obedience. The journey was hard, the journey was long, the journey was rough, and the journey was worth it!

It's worth it for you too. Stay the course, have faith and be faithful, hold onto hope and choose to trust. Immanuel is with us, and His will is worth it.

BETTER TOGETHER

Ephesians 2:19-22 "So then you are no longer strangers and aliens, but you are fellow citizens with the saints and members of the household of God, built on the foundation of the apostles and prophets, Christ Jesus himself being the cornerstone, in whom the whole structure, being joined together, grows into a holy temple in the Lord. In him you also are being built together into a dwelling place for God by the Spirit."

I love the phrase Paul uses in this portion of his letter to the Ephesians, "you are fellow citizens with the saints, and members of the household of God". I'm thinking that makes us family. For sure that's how Immanuel sees us.

Notice the plural personal pronoun "us' used in the definition of the name Immanuel? The word translated "us" is inarguably plural in its form. It means more than one and even suggests multiple.

That's not to say Immanuel isn't with ME, He is. "I will never leave YOU," is a very personal promise and one God faithfully keeps!

However, Immanuel is defined as "God with us".

We really are better together, yet there are a lot of people who feel very much alone. As the days countdown to Christmas those feelings of loneliness often intensify. Some of us will have an empty place at our house, around our table and beside our tree this holiday season. That space may be due to death, distance, or some other source of separation. Whatever the case, it can make this a very challenging time.

Of course, there are also those who are unable to go home for the holidays, or maybe have no place to go home to. If you don't have an empty space, maybe you should make one, and if you have one, consider filling it with someone who needs a place to call home for the holidays.

Because after all, He's not just Immanuel, but He's Immanuel - God with US, and we really are better together.

THE LONG ARM OF THE LORD

When I was a kid I loved watching a good western movie with my dad. The long arm of the law was sure to be found bringing justice to the desolate and desperate wilderness of the Wild West. No desperado was safe when the noble lawman was on the job. Honestly, I still love a good western.

Of course, the problem with my love of justice is that I myself would suffer judgment under its legal application. The law alone could never save.

The Scriptures pronounce in no uncertain terms that every human being stands guilty before God--guilty not only of misdemeanors, but guilty also of untold felonies. In one place it is written, "If we say we have no sin we deceive ourselves, and the truth is not in us." (1 John 1:8) And in another place, "The LORD has looked down from heaven upon the sons of men, to see if there are any who understand, who seek after God. They have all turned aside; together they have become corrupt; there is no one who does good, not even one" (Psalm 14:2-3). And God says, "For whoever keeps the whole law and yet stumbles in one point, he has become guilty of it all" (James 2:10).

Even an awareness of guilt would leave us guilty if it were not for the grace of the Savior who saves. Grace is simultaneously a revelation of our lack and His provision. The distance sin, or situation, creates between us and our Savior is precisely why he came. Immanuel covered a great distance to be with us!

Isaiah 59:1 (NASB) "Behold, the LORD's hand is not so short that it cannot save…"

The long arm of the Lord can reach into the deepest, darkness, and most desolate wilderness, and it comes to hold you not to hurt you…

Isaiah 30:18 "Therefore the Lord waits to be gracious to you, and therefore he exalts himself to show mercy to you. For the Lord is a God of justice; blessed are all those who wait for him."

WHAT A BEAUTIFUL NAME

We are under 30 days! Now everyone can get out their Christmas music and put up the decorations!

I love Christmas and I especially love the name Immanuel. Of course there's no one in history that has been given more names or titles than Jesus Christ. Over 100 names and titles, and whether He is called "Bright morning star, Wonderful Counselor, the Root of Jesse, the Alpha and the Omega, or the Lamb of God", each of these names and titles is rich with meaning. They all say something significant about who Jesus is.

However, there is no name more significant than "Immanuel". Matthew refers to Jesus as Immanuel in Matthew 1:23, but the name was first given to Jesus by the prophet Isaiah 700 years before His birth (Isaiah 7:14). And this Christmas name, as Matthew tells us, means "God with us."

Jesus is Immanuel, "God with us." The babe born to Mary in a manger, the infant that the shepherds ran to see, the newborn child that the Magi traveled hundreds of miles to worship is Immanuel, God with us. But in what sense is Jesus "God with us?"

Wasn't God always with the human race? Wasn't "God with us" before Jesus? Yes. In one sense God, the Creator, has always been "with" His creation. Unlike the false god of the Deists and Theists and of many evolutionists, who believe in a god who started the world and then departed far away, the true God has always been with us.

In Jeremiah 23 God clarifies His closeness "'Am I God who is near,' declares the LORD, 'And not far off? Can a man hide himself in hiding places, so I do not see him?' declares the LORD. 'Do I not fill the heavens and the earth?' declares the LORD." (Jer. 23:23-24 NASB)

The God of the Bible, the true Creator is omnipresent, everywhere at the same time. He fills all of creation with His presence; every mountain and every molecule; and yet He is not a part of that creation. He remains Creator distinct from His creation. And so a God who is everywhere is certainly a God who is with us.

But with the birth of Jesus in Bethlehem, Immanuel, "God With Us," took on a whole new meaning. This is the reality John wrote about.

John 1:1-3, 14 (NIV) “In the beginning was the Word, and the Word was with God, and the Word was God. He was with God in the beginning. Through him all things were made; without him nothing was made that has been made.... The Word became flesh and made his dwelling among us. We have seen his glory, the glory of the one and only Son, who came from the Father, full of grace and truth."

The great Grace of Christmas, the amazing reality: The Second Person of the Trinity, the only begotten Son of the Father, the Creator of the universe and everything and everyone in it, chose to clothe Himself in flesh, to become man, our brother, one of us. God Himself born in the manger, completely human, yet completely divine.

MEANING IN A MANGER

It's easy to forget just who the baby in the manger was. Has there ever been a more significant treasure found in a less impressive container? The omnipotent, omniscient creator of the universe was born in a stable. He spent His first night, on the planet He set in orbit, sleeping in a manger! That's just like Jesus.

1 Corinthians 1:27 "But God chose what is foolish in the world to shame the wise; God chose what is weak in the world to shame the strong."

His choice to come into such a simple setting and in such an unassuming manner was not without meaning. The manger serves as a reminder that wisdom isn't a position to be attained by accomplishment but rather a gift given to those wise enough to choose a position of humility. In fact, humility is the first and wisest choice we can make.

1 Peter 5:6 "Humble yourselves, therefore, under the mighty hand of God so that at the proper time he may exalt you."

Proverbs 1:7 "The fear of the LORD is the beginning of knowledge; fools despise wisdom and instruction."

Consider the magi from Matthew Chapter 2. Although there's much speculation and little verification about who these men were, they certainly were wise in the appreciation and respect they paid to the Christ child! They were likely members of a priestly caste of very wise men from Mesopotamia, somewhere in the east, maybe Persia or Babylon. They obviously had an understanding of astronomy and when they observed the movements of stars and planets, they recorded what they saw. When they saw the star they could not identify, they took note. More significantly, they had an understanding of Jewish prophecy. They followed both the prophecy and the star to the fulfillment of history's most important promise.

These men surpassed their own earthly wisdom and found a place in history simply by being humble enough to recognize Immanuel, the miracle from the manger, for who He was, the King of creation, in spite of His humble beginnings.

THANKFUL FOR FORGIVENESS

My family moved into the house in which I grew up when I was 2 years old. The house was not quite complete, so Mom and Dad worked on it while we lived in it.

Mom used to tell a story of the day she had just finished painting the room I shared with my brother and three older sisters. I decided I would help with decor, and I had crayons! I decided I would help by drawing a festive clown on the newly painted wall.

This was met with less approval and enthusiasm then I had anticipated! I have one of the best moms of all time, but I think she might have over-reacted a little bit. But then again, maybe not.

Either way, I got the message that what I had done was not the thing I should have done. My reaction to this revelation was to leave a note for my Mom that read, "I go away, I do bad." Don't worry, I didn't go far, I just left the note and then went to take a hot bath.

As a kid, I sometimes struggled to separate disapproval with bad behavior from disapproval with me. Some of us still struggle with that.

The truth is that no one has ever been more unconditionally and effectively loved than me. My Mom quickly corrected my misinterpretation of her correction. Even as I helped remove the poorly drawn clown, I knew I was much loved and completely forgiven. I also knew drawing on the wall was a bad idea.

Jesus didn't come so we could deny our shortcomings, paint over them, or punish us unjustly for them. He came to forgive them and restore us. Paul wrote about this to Timothy.

1 Timothy 1:15 “The saying is trustworthy and deserving of full acceptance, that Christ Jesus came into the world to save sinners, of whom I am the foremost.”

The right reaction to our failure isn't self-denial, nor is it self-loathing. It's to come to Jesus with a repentant hopeful heart for healing and restoration.

Maybe you've written that note, "I go away, I do bad" not with hand on paper, but rather in your heart.

Immanuel came to reconcile and redeem hearts and that's what He did. Don't miss that memo!

WISE MEN STILL SEEK HIM

Matthew 2:1-2 “Now after Jesus was born in Bethlehem of Judea in the days of Herod the king, behold, wise men from the east came to Jerusalem, saying, “Where is he who has been born king of the Jews? For we saw his star when it rose and have come to worship him.”

Makes me ask the introspective question, what have I "come to worship?" One thing is for sure. Wise men still seek Him!

It sure is true what Jesus said, in Matthew 6:21 “Where your treasure is, there your heart will be also”.

Sadly we often seek and search for what can only be found in Jesus everywhere but in Jesus. What do you find yourself stressing about or straining for? I'm not saying we won't have to work hard or even face struggle. Of course we will!

What I am saying is that we can spend the energy of our soul on what matters, knowing Him and making Him known. In fact, we shouldn't spend that energy on anything else.

Ultimately, the thing the Wise men were spending their energy, time and resources on was simply to see this Messiah, this Jesus, the eternal King. That’s a great investment for us to make as well. No doubt whatever we need we’ll find in Him.

If you need help, seek the Eternally Helpful.

If you need hope, seek the one Paul called the "Blessed Hope".

If you need instruction, seek the Instructor.

If you need direction, seek the Director.

What we need this Christmas season and every other day of the year, is real deal communion, fellowship, and friendship with the creator of everything. Jesus of Nazareth, born in a Bethlehem stable about 2000 years ago is Immanuel, God with us. Know this - WISE MEN STILL SEEK HIM!

BELONGING

Immanuel came to reconcile, to reconnect the Father with His children, so we could once again be the family of God. That's right; we are made to be family!

Key point: If you choose forgiveness, then you have fellowship.

In fact, the family of faith is the destiny of every person ever born, and in this family you belong. Check out what Paul wrote to the Ephesians. Ephesians 2:19 NET “So then you are no longer foreigners and noncitizens, but you are fellow citizens with the saints and members of God’s household."

These guys would have been considered outsiders before Immanuel came, and he came so that they too could belong. That was always God's plan, "That NONE should perish." (2 Peter 3:9, emphasis mine)

I grew up in a family of 7, which included Mom and Dad, 3 sisters and 1 brother. Mom and Dad worked really hard and we never lacked anything we needed, but I know theirs was a tough time to raise five kids.

One thing we never lacked was a sense of belonging. We lived in a small house with no central heat or air. Those weren't common in anyone’s homes at that time. Because of this, families spent a lot of time together, especially in the winter. The living room, (which was the room with the wood burning stove), was the room we lived in. Go figure! Of course this wasn't the only place life happened and it wasn't the only place we were family.

This togetherness caused a depth of relationship that is a treasure to this day. Being the youngest wasn't a bad thing either. I benefited from the sense of protection that comes from older brothers and sisters.

When I had my first date my sisters sorted me out and even blow-dried my hair in front of the box fan. They were my biggest fans when I had successes, and source of great comfort whenever I faced failure.

My brother kept an eye out for me as well and used to slip me a $20 when I headed off to college each Monday. He has become one of my closest friends and is still always finding ways to look out for his little brother. That's what families do.

We have had our issues, but even then, we've been family. We all know that we'll be there for each other no matter what happens. That's what makes us family.

Regardless of the kind of family you did or didn't grow up in, you have the choice to be a part of the greatest family ever - the family of God.

Maybe you feel like you just don't belong. Your big brother Jesus will argue strongly that you do. And He would know because He's the one who came to make that true.

Merry Christmas and welcome to the family.

DECEMBER

SHARING

God set the standard for sharing very high when He sent His own Son to earth to reconcile creation back to its Creator.

John 3:16 "For God so loved the world, that he gave his only Son, that whoever believes in him should not perish but have eternal life."

In fact, He set a precedent.

Romans 8:32 (NIV) "He who did not spare his own Son, but gave him up for us all - how will he not also, along with him, graciously give us all things?"

That sharing was the foundation for the early church and should still be today. As followers of God and members of His household, (Eph. 2:19), we are family. And families share.

Of that first church Luke wrote, "And all who believed were together and had all things in common." Acts 2:44 (World English Bible)

A big part of what made the house I grew up in a home was how we shared. We were never so much taught individual ownership, but rather about sharing. That's not to say I wasn't responsible for my things, but rather, I was taught that my things were to be shared with all. That sharing started with Mom and Dad who did without at times so we could have.

The local high school that I attended had a work program for lower income families that started in the 10th grade. My older brother and sisters (except MJ) worked at that job as a part of the custodial staff. It only equated to a couple of hours per day and paid minimum wage, but it was a bit of income. At the end of each pay period, when checks were picked up, my siblings always brought that pay home and gave it to my mom.

I don't remember there ever being any conversation about them doing that, nor was one needed. What I do remember is how I felt when I was in the 10th grade and I began working at that same job. What I also remember is how excited I was when I got that first check and I was able to contribute to our family's income.

I'm sure Mom gave us back more spending money and such than we were ever able to contribute, but that wasn't and isn't the point. The point was that we learned to share.

Matthew 10:8 "… Freely you have received, freely give."

And one last thought; we didn't just share a house, or the finances to run that house. We shared good times and bad times alike. We shared each other's burdens. We shared the lives that were lived in that house, and that's what made it a home. That's what made and makes us family.

Immanuel, God with us. He chose to come, and He chose to give up His life for us.

Romans 5:7-8 (NIV) "Very rarely will anyone die for a righteous person, though for a good person someone might possibly dare to die. But God demonstrates his own love for us in this: While we were still sinners, Christ died for us."

Immanuel was and is the greatest Christmas gift of all time. His love is a gift that we are meant to gladly receive and a gift we are meant to SHARE.

THE GOD OF COMPASSION

I want to have more of Jesus' capacity for compassion.

Immanuel is not a distant God who lives as a King in His castle overlooking the crystal sea. Rather, He is the King among His people, He is God with us.

Not only is He with us, but He also cares about us. He understands our hearts and hardships, and is compassionate toward us.

Hebrews 4:15 (NIV) "For we do not have a high priest who is unable to empathize with our weaknesses, but we have one who has been tempted in every way, just as we are—yet he did not sin."

It may be that you have, or are now walking through a hard season that you are certain no one can understand. Or maybe the enemy has caused you to feel like no one cares.

But Jesus understands us and what we encounter and endure. He faced those same sorts of circumstances. On the cross, He faced a hard and cruel fate at the hands of great injustice, and He faced it willingly.

That choice was made for our redemption, and to assure us of His understanding and empathy.

Yet, His ability to care is sourced from the unconditional love He has for us, not from what He experienced while He was on earth. In fact, His willingness to endure as He did came because of His compassion, not the other way around.

Lamentations 3:22-23 (NIV) "Because of the Lord's great love we are not consumed, for his compassions never fail. They are new every morning; great is your faithfulness."

Life can be incredibly unfair and yet we can know God knows and cares. He has a capacity for compassion that is extraordinary and life giving.

When we look to and lean on Him, He breathes the air back into our lungs, lifts our heads, and focuses our eyes on Him. It's in Him we have hope and find healing.

It's good to know that our Immanuel, He who has such a capacity for compassion, cares about you and me!

HONORED TO SERVE

Immanuel came not to be served but to serve.

Mark 10:42-45 (NIV) "Jesus called them together and said, 'You know that those who are regarded as rulers of the Gentiles lord it over them, and their high officials exercise authority over them. Not so with you. Instead, whoever wants to become great among you must be your servant, and whoever wants to be first must be slave of all. For even the Son of Man did not come to be served, but to serve, and to give his life as a ransom for many.'"

The family dinner table was a special place in our house when I was a kid. There were seven of us total, including Mom and Dad.

Our table had four chairs, one on each end, and two on one side, with a bench on the other side. Mom and Dad each had a chair, his on one end and hers on the side next to his. My sister, MJ, who had Down syndrome, got the chair next to Mom, as she was the princess of our home. That left only the one chair for the four remaining kids to fight over. Mom didn't actually let us fight; she devised an ingenious system to teach a valuable God lesson with our desire to sit in the best seat.

Simply put, it was ok to want the chair, but if you were sitting in that seat you would be obligated to serve everyone who was sitting on the bench. (This was practical, as it was tough to wiggle out from the bench when everyone was seated.) If someone on the bench needed a refill on water, you would get it for them. Or, if ketchup, salt, pepper, or anything else were needed, the person sitting in the serving chair, the best chair would get it for them.

That's why we called that best chair, the serving chair. I know that's not how it always works in the kingdom, the household of faith, but it's how it should. I presently serve alongside of some of the most humble servants and what a blessing that is to God and His church.

This Christmas let's remember what an honor it is to serve, and then let's serve. Because when we do, we are imitating Immanuel.

OBVIOUS, IN UNEXPECTED PLACES

Immanuel, God with us, has a tendency to make Himself known in some very unexpected places and to some very unsuspecting people.

This was never truer than on the night of His birth. When the angels were dispatched to announce the Messiah's arrival, they didn't do so at a party, nor did they travel to a palace, but rather they were sent to a pasture.

The shepherds they visited weren't famous, nor were they at a revival meeting. They were working the night shift on a lonely hillside outside the city. Yet they were the ones invited to the stable to celebrate the virgin birth.

Luke 2:8-11 "And in the same region there were shepherds out in the field, keeping watch over their flock by night. And an angel of the Lord appeared to them, and the glory of the Lord shone around them, and they were filled with great fear. And the angel said to them, "Fear not, for behold, I bring you good news of great joy that will be for all the people. For unto you is born this day in the city of David a Savior, who is Christ the Lord."

Obvious, in an unexpected place!

I've had this same experience; I have often seen Jesus the most clearly in the places you would have expected least to see Him.

The Three Wise Men followed the star over great distance, and at great expense, only to find that it had stopped over a stable. Not a palatial palace, but a simple stable! Yet when they got where they were going, they found themselves in the presence of the King.

The King shows up where we expect Him the least and with a love so real you can't possibly miss it.

He's made a habit of showing up in my life in places and at times when and where I was feeling alone and isolated. And He doesn't just show up incognito or under the radar, He shows up real and tangible so we can know it's Him, so we can know He's with us!

SILENT NIGHT, HOLY NIGHT

This song was written in 1818 by the young priest Father Joseph Mohr and is written about the night of Christ's birth.

Silent night, holy night

All is calm, all is bright

Round yon Virgin Mother and Child

Holy Infant so tender and mild

Sleep in heavenly peace

Sleep in heavenly peace

Really? To be completely honest, as much as I love Christmas music and carols, I sometimes question the certainty with which certain statements were made.

I remember as a kid wondering how we could make such assumptions about the night Jesus was born. I'm thinking this night seemed a bit chaotic, at least to Mary and Joseph.

Maybe my favorite "what are you talking about" lyric comes from *Away in a Manger*:

The cattle are lowing

The poor Baby wakes

But little, Lord Jesus

No crying He makes

Seriously, what baby wakes up with a cow in their face and doesn't scream at the top of their lungs? And what is lowing?

I'm guessing it was a bit hectic though, especially for Joseph and Mary. I know I get in trouble if our travel plans are not well laid out. Why didn't Joseph phone ahead and at least make a motel reservation?

Obviously, I'm being facetious. But what I do know is that the Messiah was born in a stable. That Mary gave birth without a doctor or a midwife, and the only nurses were the on-looking livestock.

Luke 2:6-7 "And while they were there, the time came for her to give birth. And she gave birth to her firstborn son and wrapped him in swaddling cloths and laid him in a manger, because there was no place for them in the inn."

Mary and Joseph were seeing the fulfillment of a promise God made, not only to them, but also to and for all creation. However, the way that promise was working out must have seemed a bit hectic. Maybe, even in jeopardy!

I've certainly felt that way about God's purposes and plans in my own life, and I've never been responsible for birthing or raising the Redeemer of the world.

I'm guessing if Mary and Joseph wrote their own Christmas carol recounting the night of Christ birth, it would be about God's presence and peace despite the unexpected. Maybe there would be an honest verse expressing the difficulty and then a bridge describing the beauty of God's faithfulness and the contentedness that comes from knowing He is Immanuel, God with us.

DO YOU SEE WHAT I SEE? PART 1

We're meant to see what's going on in the world around us. We're meant to see and notice people, and to make sure they know they're noticed by God.

As I was writing today's devotion at a local coffee shop, I had strategic God interactions with a couple of different people with whom I had no standing appointments. I guess that's not strictly true. Apparently, I had divine appointments with them both.

The first was with a fellow God follower who had lost an uncle and was on his way to the funeral. He was a believer who simply needed a practical hands-on reminder that God is with him.

The second was with a lady I hadn't seen in years. She used to own and operate my favorite Mexican restaurant. As soon as she walked through I realized Immanuel wanted to bless her with kindness and concern and I would be His messenger. We chatted about old times, good food, and a gracious God. She needs Jesus! She needs relationships with ladies who know Jesus. She needs to know Jesus is for her and with her. I was able to communicate all of that in one God directed 20-minute conversation.

I think divine appointments are a lot more common than we think. Either that or God is bad at math. For sure there are lots of people in our world of interaction each day who need more than a casual hello. In fact, our lives are full of people who need a real-life representation of the love God has for them. That's a representation we are meant to be if we will choose to see.

My wife, Karen, and I pray every morning before we roll out of bed that we will be on point with what matters to God. We pray that He will cause us to see. It's no surprise Jesus loves to answer that prayer. After all, it's Immanuel who makes us alive and aware. As He's working in us, He's also working through us, causing us to see and to care.

So get those eyes open and your heart ready. Immanuel wants to be God through you. Do you see what I see?

John 4:35 "Do you not say, 'There are yet four months, then comes the harvest?' Look, I tell you, lift up your eyes, and see that the fields are white for harvest."

DO YOU SEE WHAT I SEE? PART 2

Do you remember the old axiom, what you see is what you get?

There is some significant truth in that statement. I'm not saying that we can call things into existence that aren't there, nor am I a fan of any "name it, claim it" theology.

What I am saying, is that we often miss the good things God is doing in and around us simply because we fail to see. In fact, we may be choosing to see only one side of our situation.

For instance, it's easy to see the trouble without seeing the very present help.

Psalms 46:1 "God is our refuge and strength, a very present help in trouble."

I understand this. Trouble can create such a cloud of confusion that we may struggle to see what we know is there. Maybe, the most significant trouble with trouble is that it can cause us to forget the truth.

John 16:33 "I have said these things to you, that in me you may have peace. In the world you will have tribulation. But take heart; I have overcome the world."

Do you see what I see? I see all sorts of problems and pain, but I also see God marvelously present in the midst of them. I see a Messiah who came to love and to liberate, a Messiah who didn't avoid difficulty but faced it for us.

I see hurt, and I see hope. I see Immanuel, God with us.

Do you see what I see?

I'LL SEE IT WHEN I BELIEVE IT!

Yesterday's devotional centered on a not-so-subtle reminder that truth and trouble aren't mutually exclusive. Immanuel is "an ever-present help".

The key point: Trouble isn't an evidence of God's absence, but comes with a promise of His presence.

Still, no matter how much we know that truth in our heads, it can be very hard to see in our hearts.

My friend Rick Hickman rightly commented on yesterday's devotional, "I'll see it when I believe it". Believing is seeing. Do you see what I see?!

It takes faith in His nature and character, in His immutable love, and in His limitless grace to see. It takes faith in His promise of faithfulness, and in the promise of forever, to give us His eternal perspective in spite of our problems.

Faith has always been the way God does His work.

Hebrew 11:1-3 "Now faith is the assurance of things hoped for, the conviction of things not seen. For by it the people of old received their commendation. By faith we understand that the universe was created by the word of God, so that what is seen was not made out of things that are visible."

Don't worry, you don't need to create a universe, you just need to believe He did. You don't need to save the world; you just need to believe He has. And, you don't have to heal your heart; you just need to believe that He can.

And don't panic about not having enough faith. Lack of faith is rarely the issue. Trying to have enough faith is often the same as putting our faith in our faith. Rather, take the faith you have and put it in our great big God. He's given each of us an "allotment of faith" and even "faith the size of a mustard seed" when applied to Him is enough for major spiritual landscaping! (Romans 12:3 & Matthew 17:21)

Faith isn't our way to tell God what to do. It's the way we connect with what He's done.

The Christmas story tells us of a man named Simeon who was waiting for the arrival of the Messiah. Luke tells us he was righteous and devout, and the Holy Spirit was upon him. He was waiting to see the promised Messiah, and he did, because he believed.

Luke 2:30-32 "For my eyes have seen your salvation, which you have prepared in the sight of all people, a light for revelation to the Gentiles and for glory to your people Israel."

Simeon saw because He believed. God help us believe too. Help us see because we choose the grace to believe, to believe that you ARE Immanuel, God with us.

MASTER BUILDER

Matthew 1:23 (World English Bible) "Behold, a virgin shall be with child, and shall bring forth a son, and they shall call his name Immanuel, which being interpreted is, God with us."

Jesus' adopted father Joseph was a builder, maybe a carpenter, maybe a stone mason, but definitely a builder. (Matthew 13:55; Mark 6:3). The Greek word is used to describe Joseph's profession is *teckton* which means builder.

Jewish boys learned the trade of their fathers by the age of 12. I'm sure Jesus learned building from Joseph.

Why does this matter? Because when Immanuel came, he came not only as a baby in a manger, but also as a builder with a blue print and a hard hat.

Paul gives a description of Immanuel in his letter to the Hebrews which sounds a lot like that of an architect and a builder.

Hebrews 12:2 "Let us fix our eyes on Jesus, the author and finisher of our faith..."

So what does He design and build? Author and finish? Paul gave us an answer to that question. He builds our faith, or even more specifically our life of faith. That's one house we can't build without Him, and a house that will only stand when built by Him.

The Psalmist was so certain of this reality that he said in Psalm 127:1 "Unless the LORD builds the house, the builders labor in vain".

Can I encourage you today to trust in who He is and the heart He has for you? His plans for you stretch into eternity and are kept safe in the hands of Messiah, the master builder.

As Paul wrote to the Philippians, He who began a good work in you will be faithful to complete it... (Phil 1:6)

Faithful, capable, compassionate, and for us! Immanuel, God with us.

HE GAVE

John 3:16 "For God so loved the world that He gave…"

One of the more significant challenges of the Christmas season can be as simple as discerning what to get the people on your list. This is especially true if you've become a little disconnected from their current likes, wants or needs. Of course, the best gifts are the ones that say the giver knows what you want and what you need.

Clearly, the greatest gift of all time was the first Christmas gift when God gave His son and when Jesus chose to come; He gave His life so we could have life. He was the one gift we couldn't live without.

The fact is Jesus came on and with a mission. He came to shatter the false image of a distant and disinterested God whose only aim was to judge and punish. He came fully aware of what we needed and that is the gift He gave.

John 3:17 (NIV) "For God did not send his Son into the world to condemn the world, but to save the world through Him."

I John 4:14 (NASB) "We have seen and testify that the Father has sent the Son to be the Savior of the world."

His heart and passion were and are to demonstrate the love of God to every person on the planet. He actually came for the very people who rejected Him.

He touched the lepers, the lame and the sick that others avoided. He had lunch with tax collectors and prostitutes. He gave compassion where others offered only condemnation.

His default reaction toward the imperfect was grace and mercy while He reserved His harsh words for the impertinent, and those who hated the hurting and oppressed the needy. His only anger was with anyone who would stand in the way of the Father's desire to rescue, and restore broken people.

Romans 5:8 "God shows his love for us in that while we were still sinners, Christ died for us."

His love was more than sentiment. He took action and initiative to connect with you and me, to touch and heal our hearts and redeem our lives.

He came to give and He gave. He gave Himself, and that's what makes Him Immanuel, God with us.

THE LITTLE BIG PRINCIPLE

It never ceases to amaze me just how quickly little things can add up. This can be in both the positive and the negative sense. The change from my pocket piles up in my dresser drawer and in no time becomes enough to treat a friend to lunch. On the other hand, a few seemingly small impulse buys can make you wonder where your money went. It all adds up, hence the saying "It's the little things that count".

The Great Chicago Fire occurred in 1871. As the story goes, a cow in Mrs. O'Leary's barn kicked over a lamp. That lamp broke and caught a wisp of hay on fire. Soon, the whole barn was up in flames, which then spread to and consumed the city. Hundreds of people died and millions of dollars of damage occurred, all from a kicking cow.

Little things can become huge, and quickly, or they can cause a slow burn that, in the end, still does significant damage.

Big things add up too and even more quickly, but that's no great surprise or revelation. However, the little things often get little attention and may even do their damage with little awareness, leaving us to wonder where our peace and joy went and how it took us so long to notice it was gone.

Little things come in the form of every day challenges and frustrations. They're empty milk containers and cereal boxes. They're lost backpacks, purses, wallets, keys, and cell phones. They're a car that won't start, traffic that doesn't move, and a boss that won't budge. Little things can be big challenges when we allow them to rule our days, and rob us of our peace and joy.

I know for many of you these little challenges would be a welcomed respite from your daily battle. But like everyone else, I have some "big" things that aren't right in my life too. However, when I keep the peace and walk in joy, the grace is there for "all things," no matter their size or significance.

I know you know that for those who love God all things work together for good… Romans 8:28

And here's my favorite revelation about little things making a big difference: 2000 or so years ago a "little baby" was born in a "little village," in a "little stable," and that has made a HUGE difference. It made all the difference in the world.

Luke 2:4-7 (NIV) "So Joseph also went up from the town of Nazareth in Galilee to Judea, to Bethlehem the town of David, because he belonged to the house and line of David. He went there to register with Mary, who was pledged to be married to him and was expecting a child. While they were there, the time came for the baby to be born, and she gave birth to her firstborn, a son. She wrapped him in cloths and placed him in a manger, because there was no guest room available for them."

This little baby boy, made a big difference. Immanuel, God with us.

JOY TO THE WORLD, THE LORD HAS COME!

Matthew 2:10 "When they saw the star, they rejoiced exceedingly with great joy."

Immanuel's coming brought with it great joy. Because He came, we can have joy too. I'm not saying we will always be happy. I know that you know there's a big difference between joy and happiness.

The root word for joy in biblical Greek is *Chara*. It's a noun defined as joy, or gladness, literally the joy received from God. Happy, on the other hand, comes from the root word *hap* for happenstance.

As the days to Christmas become fewer and fewer, I know for some the weight becomes heavier and heavier. I'm praying that we will all choose joy. I'm fully aware that this time of year can, for some, be the most difficult season of all. That's one of the reasons I wrote this countdown devotional.

I'm also completely certain that God's heart for us is joy, His joy. I'm not saying we've been promised happiness, but I am saying He came so we could have joy in all seasons and circumstances.

Yet, if we're honest, there are thoughts, or triggers, which take us back to a place of anxiety that, in a moment, can rob us of our joy. Anxiety has many sources – worry, busyness, grief, transition, and relational tension, to name a few. All of these can be intensified during the holiday season.

Remember joy has triggers too, such as friendship, thankfulness, faith, hope, and presence; especially His presence.

Romans 15:13 (LEB) "May the God of hope fill you with all joy and peace in believing, so that you may abound in hope by the power of the Holy Spirit."

1 Peter 5:6-7 (NIV) "Humble yourselves, therefore, under God's mighty hand, that he may lift you up in due time. Cast all your anxiety on him because he cares for you."

No doubt, now more than ever our focus should be on Immanuel, God with us. Because, "in His presence is fullness of joy." Psalms 16:11. JOY TO THE WORLD, THE LORD HAS COME…

ALL THINGS NEW

What's wrong with this world? Come on, I know you've noticed. Don't misunderstand. I'm blessed and I know it. There are so many things I enjoy and appreciate about God's amazing creation, but I'm not naïve either. I'm fully aware that it's not all good and often it's very bad.

In physics there's a concept known as entropy that applies or relates to the Laws of Thermodynamics. Simply put, this concept says that things in a closed system move from a state of order to disorder. Isaac Asimov summarized it saying, "All we have to do is nothing, and everything deteriorates, collapses, breaks down, wears out, all by itself—and that is what entropy and the second law of thermodynamics is all about."

Without outside influence or input, things don't become more ordered, they become less ordered. I'll readily admit that this is an oversimplification, but the concept is one that applies across the board in God's created world.

In the universe, cycle is no doubt a part of God's creative plan. In the spiritual world and in the human context, chaos, death, and destruction, were not part of the original design. We know that those things came as a result of the Fall and have been going on since sin entered the world in the garden.

Genesis 2:17 "But of the tree of the knowledge of good and evil you shall not eat, for in the day that you eat of it you shall surely die."

Entropy can be overcome though. It takes an outside influence and an application of energy or work. A random pile of bricks can't become a wall without the hand of a skilled mason. Neither can an old and broken down car become a valuable classic without the restorative work of a gifted mechanic and body technician.

Romans 6:23 "For the wages of sin is death, but the free gift of God is eternal life in Christ Jesus our Lord."

The damage the Fall has done in our world is obvious. We've all experienced its impact. We need the help that can only come from outside of this world, and yet the work could only be done from within. That's why Immanuel came. He came from outside the system to work inside the system, to restore the system, to restore us.

Romans 5:17 (NLT) "For the sin of this one man, Adam, caused death to rule over many. But even greater is God's wonderful grace and his gift of righteousness, for all who receive it will live in triumph over sin and death through this one man, Jesus Christ."

This isn't a work we can do ourselves. Our ONLY hope is for an outside intervention. You can try all you want to just be better, or to make it go away. You can pretend for everyone else or maybe even for yourself that everything's ok, but we all know hurt is real. Hopelessness can be a burden that never leaves, but hope HAS come and His name is Immanuel.

Choose that! Choose Him! He came to make ALL things new. The baby in the manger is the God of restoration. We're so much more than projects to Him; we're His priority. We're why He came. He came to make us new.

One day the world won't be broken. But until then we have Immanuel, God with us, making all things new.

Revelation 21:3-5 (NASB) "And I heard a loud voice from the throne, saying, 'Behold, the tabernacle of God is among men, and He will dwell among them, and they shall be His people, and God Himself will be among them, and He will wipe away every tear from their eyes; and there will no longer be any death; there will no longer be any mourning, or crying, or pain; the first things have passed away.' And He who sits on the throne said, 'Behold, I am making all things new.' And He said, Write, for these words are faithful and true.'"

THE LOSS OF THE INNOCENT AND THE LOSS OF INNOCENCE

(I originally wrote this devotion on December 14, 2012 the day of the Sandy Hook school shooting in Newtown, CT. It was the hardest day for me to write and yet it is the devotional that, for me, means the most.)

Today's news of the school shooting and consequent deaths of truly innocent lives in Newtown, CT. has been a devastating reminder of how dark darkness can be.

Mortality is a harsh reminder of our fragility, and cruelty an even harsher reminder of our depravity. I'm writing this devotion from our apartment here in Blacksburg, Virginia and less than a mile from the Virginia Tech campus. The community here still feels the hurt from our own tragic day back in April 2007, when 32 students and faculty were shot and killed.

I must admit days like this are beyond description. I can't, nor will I try, to find words that explain a pain beyond description. The death of children is the worst kind of injustice, and yet it's not a new attack of the enemy. In an attempt to wipe out Immanuel, the evil King Herod killed every Jewish boy under the age of two who was living in the vicinity of Jerusalem, an unthinkable atrocity!

Matthew 2:16-18 (NIV) "When Herod realized that he had been outwitted by the Magi, he was furious, and he gave orders to kill all the boys in Bethlehem and its vicinity who were two years old and under, in accordance with the time he had learned from the Magi. Then what was said through the prophet Jeremiah was fulfilled: 'A voice is heard in Ramah, weeping and great mourning, Rachel weeping for her children and refusing to be comforted, because they are no more.'"

This is the mourning we feel today; a mourning that knows no comfort, but a mourning that must find hope.

Although baby Jesus was spared the plot of this murderous mad man, He would later die a willing and redemptive death for the children who died before Him and all who have died since. Hope came into this hard and hateful place to bring life in the face of death, to bring healing in the midst of deep pain, and to hold the hearts of those devastated by death's evil impact. That hope can only be of the eter nal variety, as no other hope will suffice, and that hope can only be found in Immanuel.

The kind of evil that was carried out today, and the evil of 2000 Christmases ago, are beyond comprehension and will NEVER be okay, nor explained away.

I could take you through a dissertation on God's love, free will, the effects of the fall, and the depravity of man, and when we were done I would feel no more comforted than I do now, and neither would you. It's just not okay for parents to be left without their children.

And yet I KNOW my heavenly Father sent His own Son to die so that one-day death too would die. Even now we know that for the child, and for the child of God, death is a miraculous segue into eternal life. Today that may seem like little consolation, and in fact it's no consolation at all. But it is hope, eternal hope! A hope that stands through the long dark night and a Hope that's hand delivered to every hurting heart by Immanuel Himself, God with us.

WHAT A FRIEND WE HAVE IN JESUS

Indeed, we do have a hope that has been hand delivered by Immanuel. He said Himself in John 14:6, "I am the way, the truth, and the life…" And in John 15:15 Jesus said to His followers, "I have called you friends..."

Can we find a friend so faithful, who will all our sorrows share?

Jesus knows our every weakness; take it to the Lord in prayer.

Are we weak and heavy laden, cumbered with a load of care?

Precious Savior, still our refuge; take it to the Lord in prayer.

The hymn writer Joseph Scriven, penned this truth in the song "What a Friend We Have in Jesus." Scriven came to Jesus after losing his bride-to-be on the eve of their marriage. An unbelievable grief for sure! The evidence of God's presence even in this tragedy can be found in the last lines of verse three: "In His arms He'll take and shield thee; Thou wilt find a solace there".

The same God who was with Daniel in the lion's den, and with Shadrach, Meshach, and Abednego in the fiery furnace, was also with John the Baptist at his execution, and ministered eternal hope to a dying thief moments before His own death on the cross

It's that manifest presence of God in all things that has given strength to people facing every kind of difficulty, from the devastating effects of sickness, sorrow, or even martyrdom. "In His arms."

Micah 7:7 "But as for me, I will look to the Lord; I will wait for the God of my salvation; my God will hear me."

Great grief can make you feel isolated and alone. How can anyone understand the depth of the heartache and hurt? Maybe you know this sense of isolation first hand. I hope you also know that there's an even deeper reality, no matter how we feel, or what we face, God IS with us.

Psalm 147:3 "He heals the brokenhearted and binds up their wounds."

Psalm 34:18 "The Lord is near to the brokenhearted and saves the crushed in spirit."

Immanuel God with us, what a friend!

A LIGHT IN THE DARKNESS

Darkness is something we've all experienced, both figuratively and literally. It's a very hectic environment to be sure. I've had some pretty crazy accidents in the dark.

One of my all-time worst bicycle wrecks happened on a dark night. I went camping with a couple of my best high school buddies, Chris Hackler and Kenny Williams. Kenny and I were abnormally small for our age; in fact, our nicknames were Skinny Kenny and Scrawny Ronnie. Because of our diminutive size we were riding 20 inch one-speed bicycles. Regular size Chris on the other hand was riding a full-size ten-speed bicycle making it a bit difficult for Kenny and me to keep up.

Our destination took us down a rural country highway that had no lighting. Additionally, it was a very dark moonless and cloudy night. In other words, we couldn't see very far in front of ourselves. At one point Kenny and I decided to give it all we had to catch up with Chris who at this point had disappeared into the darkness. As we gained speed pushing our little legs and bicycles to their limits, Chris suddenly appeared out of the darkness where he was waiting broadside in Kenny's lane. The crash when they collided full on was of cataclysmic proportions. In fact, Chris's ten-speed was now a no-speed, with a broken frame at the rear sprocket! The two of them were less than happy with each other, and I was just relieved that neither was seriously hurt.

The worst though is when you're startled out of bed in the middle of the night with no time to turn on the light. Running through the house, half asleep, in a careless panic, and with no light, is a sure recipe for disaster!

Unfortunately, much of the darkness we encounter is of a more significant nature. Our days can be full of uncertainties and difficulties that leave us struggling to see.

This life, and all that comes with it, can certainly leave us startled and struggling to navigate the darkness, sometimes in a panic. The how and why questions, even when answered, often only lead to more questions.

The best plan in a dark-time crisis is to push forward with careful resolve. Let your heart and eyes adjust and find the light. No matter how dark the darkness, there is always light.

John 1:5 "The light shines in the darkness, and the darkness has not overcome it."

Luke 2:8-11 "And in the same region there were shepherds out in the field, keeping watch over their flock by night. And an angel of the Lord appeared to them, and THE GLORY OF THE LORD SHONE AROUND THEM, and they were filled with great fear. And the angel said to them, "Fear not, for behold, I bring you good news of great joy that will be for all the people.

For unto you is born this day in the city of David a SAVIOR, who is Christ the Lord" (Emphasis mine).

The revelation of Christ's birth was announced with a manifestation of light that could only be described as "the Glory of the Lord." The great revelation was the birth of a "Savior." A Savior we so need, and need to see. He is our hope, our help, and our healing. He is Immanuel, God with us.

GOD'S GOT A GREAT GRIP!

Hebrews 13:5 "I will never leave you nor forsake you".

That promise is found over and over in the bible, from Deuteronomy all the way to our example in Paul's letter to the Hebrews. In fact, it's made in many other forms from Genesis to Revelation.

It's as if God wants to make a point. He doesn't leave, and He doesn't let go. Hence, the "ever present help" statement in Psalm 46:1.

In difficulty, a dangerous tendency can be to just try and "toughen up", or "handle it" ourselves. We'll load up more than we could possibly ever carry, and try to muscle through.

When Jacob (my youngest son) was a kid, he was very helpful, and he still is. He and Isaac (my oldest son) would always come out and help carry in the groceries. Jacob had a habit of trying to carry way more than was possible for his little kid-sized arms. I often reminded him to not try and carry so much. Once, on grocery day, Jacob had grabbed a couple of pretty heavy bags full of cans and such. As he tried to navigate the steps through the back door, he lost it. Not only did he hit the ground, but as he did, the bags spilled and much of their contents rolled under the car or across the driveway.

You can imagine what I said to him. "Jacob, how many times have I told you? You're in so much trouble!" I hope you don't think that's what I said. I hope you believe I'm a better dad than that. What I did do was help him pick up what was spilled, scooped him and his load up and carried them into the kitchen.

Sometimes, our load is so heavy that pushing through isn't even an option. Things are so hard that we just want to give up. I've seen that as a dad too, and I've experienced it as a son.

I've had moments in life when the weight of what I was facing overwhelmed whatever strength I had. I've known the powerful hand holding me in grace, and carrying me to peace. That "knowing" was the only thing that kept me from great strain and stress, if not sheer panic.

Psalms 71:5 "For you, O LORD, are my hope, my trust, O LORD from my youth."

Dads and sons aren't always the ones carrying heavy loads. I've always been amazed at moms. Give a dad a baby to hold and pretty soon he's whining about how heavy this "little chunk" is. But the tiniest mom can hold a baby off, and on all day, while multi-tasking her way around the house and never seem fazed at all. I'm convinced God gave moms special baby-holding muscles.

What I do know for sure is that God has an inexhaustible ability to hold His children. He has baby-holding muscles. Immanuel, the God who is with us, is able to hold us and sustain us, He's got great grip.

IMMANUEL, GOD WITH US, GOD THROUGH US

I know you know I love Christmas. It's such a great time and opportunity to show who Jesus is and the love He has for us all. Knowing Him and making Him known is what we're going for here. Christmas is an easier time than most to get that done. Immanuel, God with us, is Immanuel, God through us. Check out John the Beloved's view of God's love revealed.

1 John 4:9-12 (NIV) "This is how God showed his love among us: He sent his one and only Son into the world that we might live through him. This is love: not that we loved God, but that he loved us and sent his Son as an atoning sacrifice for our sins. Dear friends, since God so loved us, we also ought to love one another. No one has ever seen God; but if we love one another, God lives in us and his love is made complete in us."

I love that His love "is made complete in us" when we "love one another." To experience His love completely we have to share His love freely. If you get all the way in, you'll be all the way wet. If you love others, you'll experience the fullness of His love.

I actually LOVE spending my days finding ways to be a revelation of His love. I'm not saying I'm super great at it, but I am super graced for it. Doing "random" things intentionally is often the best way to live strategically. God moments happen in the seemingly insignificant conversation or connection we have with a friend or family member who just needs to know they're not forgotten. Loving others happens over morning coffee, or in conversation with the stranger, or maybe across the checkout counter of a store. These moments happen at home, work, school, or wherever we are found being who we are, and doing what we always do.

They happen with eyes and heart open to Him and to others. And this time of year, they happen by serving, sharing, and seeing the needs and opportunities this unique season offers. They happen when we live the reality that Immanuel is God with us and, simultaneously, God through us!

PA RUM PUM PUM PUM

I love cartoons, and I especially love Christmas cartoons. The classics are the best! "Frosty the Snow Man," "Rudolph the Red-Nosed Reindeer," "Santa Claus is Coming to Town," and all the ones with Chris Kringle, are some of my favorites. But my top three are, "A Charlie Brown Christmas," "The Grinch that Stole Christmas," and my number one is…"The Little Drummer Boy."

This old school stop motion was produced by Rankin/Bass and based on the 1941 song of the same name written by Katherine K. Davis. It originally aired December 19, 1968 on NBC, where it was shown every Christmas for several years. And yes, I did say December 19th, which in 1968 was my 4th birthday. That's the first birthday from which I have memories, and as silly as it may sound, this simple cartoon impacted my thinking.

The story centers on a little farm boy named Aaron who is orphaned when his home is burned and his parents are killed by bandits from the desert. His heart filled with hatred, Aaron vows to avoid contact will all humans. Finding companionship with three farm animals that survived the attack, he sets out on his own. Yet through a series of events beyond his control, Aaron finds himself following a star to Bethlehem. He travels the same path taken by three earthly kings, or "Wise Men," who are following a prophetic vision about the birth of an eternal King. A chariot hits Aaron's little lamb, Baabaa, just as they arrive in Bethlehem. In desperation he approaches one of the kings for help, only to find himself standing at the manger where Jesus has been born. Realizing the need to give this newborn King a gift, and with nothing in hand, he offers the only thing he has, a song on his drum.

"Little Baby, pa rum pum pum pum.

I am a poor boy too, pa rum pum pum pum.

I have no gift to bring… that's fit to give our King…

Shall I play for you, pa rum pum pum pum, on my drum? "

I can relate to Aaron. As a kid I often identified myself more by what I lacked than by what I had. The youngest of five, I grew up in a small church and went to a very small school in a very small town. I saw myself as having no impressive talent or resource. I wondered what I could possibly offer in service to my Savior and King.

I know this story doesn't come from the Bible, but it certainly represents the heart Jesus has for those of us who see ourselves or what we bring to the kingdom as insignificant. Sometimes it's others who help to form our low opinion of what we have to add. Regardless of the source or voice, it's certainly not true and it's certainly not God. We're not alone in this inaccurate value assessment. The list of Bible heroes who were seen or saw themselves as unimportant and un-impactful is long and impressive. Let's give it a quick and synoptic look: Moses, Joshua, Rahab, Gideon, Ruth, David, Mary the mother of Jesus, Mary Magdalene, and all twelve of the disciples of Jesus fit our description. Yet each of these, like each of us, were simply called to live and give our lives to the one who gave Himself for us. We're called to play our drum with and for Him. "Pa Rum Pum Pum Pum."

As my sister, MJ, used to say, "I was born on my birthday, and for me this is that day." When I was a kid I didn't see me being born any big deal. I loved my family and I loved being alive, but I didn't value the fact that God valued me. The beautiful truth is everyone is a big deal to Immanuel, that's why He's with us! He's for us. He values who we are and He values what we bring!

Every courtesy and unseen act of kindness is a big deal to God. "Pa Rum Pum Pum Pum." Every moment of integrity and honesty, every day of faithful friendship, every effort to grow in grace and to show His grace is a gift back to the God who gave it all. "Pa Rum Pum Pum Pum." I was made to play, to play my part, to play my drum for Him!

"Mary nodded, Pa Rum Pum Pum Pum

The ox and lamb kept time, Pa Rum Pum Pum Pum

I played my drum for Him... I played my best for Him...

Then He smiled at me, Pa Rum Pum Pum Pum, me and my drum."

CHRISTMAS PRESENCE

With only five days until Christmas left, there's a good chance you've either made or bought a gift or two. Homemade or customized presents are my favorite, but if you want to buy me something that's ok too. As much I enjoyed Christmas as a kid, I've enjoyed it even more as a dad. Karen and I have loved buying, making, and giving Isaac and Jacob all sorts of presents and surprises over the years, noticing that the getting experience seemed as important as what was gotten.

Often when we think about Christmas, the first things that come to mind are the presents and the family gatherings with all that amazing food. However, as much as I enjoy gifts and goodies, Christmas is actually much more about the presence than the presents.

Exodus 33:14 "And he said, 'My presence will go with you, and I will give you rest.'"

I never cease to be amazed at the faithfulness of God and His presence in our lives. He certainly gives us gifts or "presents" as well. He is our provider in every sense of the word, meeting physical, emotional and spiritual needs. FYI, He meets "needs" which are not the same as "wants." "God with us" isn't a promise of prosperity, but it's certainly a promise of provision and presence. Immanuel is faithfully present.

I'm sure Isaac and Jacob have appreciated all the Christmas presents we've gotten them, but I think it's our presence in their lives all year long that has been the biggest blessing. We can't keep life from happening or from happening to them, but we can be there for each other 365 days a year.

That's how it is with Immanuel. His presence doesn't restrict The Fall from having a negative impact on our lives, but it does ensure we can choose redemption even in the worst situations. Life can be very unpredictable, and yet the march toward Christmas reminds us that as surely as the sun rises and sets every day, God is on His throne and on our side. His presence isn't just a Christmas thing, it's a God thing and that's a good thing!

REFLECTION = REDEMPTION

John 1:6-8 “There was a man sent from God, whose name was John. He came as a witness, to bear witness about the light, that all might believe through him. He was not the light, but came to bear witness about the light.”

I'm not the light, but I'm certainly a reflection of the light. I don't run around trying to be Jesus, but I sure do want to be like Jesus. I'm meant to be like Jesus.

In fact, we're all meant to reflect the nature and character of Christ, to shine His light in the darkness, and when we do, redemption happens. Redemption happens in the lives of other people, and redemption happens in our hearts. This Christmas season, many of us are dealing with loss and hurt, and all of us can relate. None of us are beyond the need for redemption.

We search for answers to questions that are too big for us. We hope for a hope we hardly believe is possible, and yet somehow it grows and gains ground in our hearts.

For the better part of three months, we've been sharing this time and space to consider the power of God's faithfulness. I've been working with Immanuel to remind us all of how HE IS WITH US! These past four days we've been more specifically considering how HE IS ALSO THROUGH US.

Can I now remind you that those two truths are inextricably linked? As Jeremiah wrote in Chapter 20, verse 9, "his word is in my heart like a fire, a fire shut up in my bones. I am weary of holding it in; indeed, I cannot."

Out of the abundance of the heart the mouth speaks. When God is doing work in you, it will work its way out in word and deed.

Words are a whisper until they’re amplified by action, but when people can tell you care, they will care about what you tell, or have to say. And when what we say is based on the common experience that life brings, the good and bad we’ve experienced find redemption in the help and hope they give to others.

Your hurt isn't a liability to your testimony. Cynicism is, bitterness is, but hurting isn't. Hurting and hoping are not mutually exclusive!

You don't have to wait for the fullness of healing to come for you to bring help to others. It's often in helping that we find our own path to hope and healing. It's in REFLECTION, that we find REDEMPTION.

It's when we share honestly and hopefully that we can reflect the light we've found in darkness.

Immanuel God with us, God through us.

WE ARE WHY HE CAME!

I wonder if the devil saw Him coming. I know he knew the prophecies, but did he believe He would really come? For all the knowledge he had, he clearly didn't understand God. Otherwise, he would never have tried that whole "hostile takeover" thing that started this mess in the first place.

After watching Jesus for tens of thousands of years, he must have had some idea of how much He loved humanity. But still, did he believe He would actually enter it to save it? That's just what He did. Maybe Satan even asked Jesus, "What are YOU doing here?" Whatever the case, He came, and in doing so He clearly communicated why. We are why He came.

Matthew 18:11-12 (NASB) "For the Son of Man has come to save that which was lost." What do you think? If any man has a hundred sheep, and one of them has gone astray, does he not leave the ninety nine on the mountains and go and search for the one that is straying?"

He came so that not one would be lost, at least not without the option to be found. He not only made an eternal plan for redemption, He was the plan. We are why He came.

Yet as I'm writing this devotional here at Starbucks, I'm overhearing the compassionate conversation of one man chatting to another. The first man, near my age, is chatting to a younger man, maybe thirty or so. It's clear from the conversation that the younger man has lost his wife during this last year. It's also clear that he has daughters. They're talking about life, finances, school, and Christmas. The conversation is real, deep, but not heavy.

He came for the lost, and He came for the living. We are why He came.

I knew God's presence was a bit more obvious this morning, but I wasn't sure why. Now I know. He's following this young father closely these days. The conversation I'm hearing has a redemptive tone, a steady strength, and a peace that's pushing through the pain. Those can only come from an "ever-present help," and an "Eternal Hope."

John 14:1-6 "Let not your hearts be troubled. Believe in God; believe also in me. In my Father's house are many rooms. If it were not so, would I have told you that I go to prepare a place for you? And if I go and prepare a place for you, I will come again and will take you myself, that where I am you may be also. And you know the way to where I am going." Thomas said to him, "Lord, we do not know where you are going. How can we know the way?" Jesus said to him, "I am the way, and the truth, and the life. No one comes to the Father except through me."

I recognize God's presence at the table next to mine because I myself have needed it and I myself have experienced it. That's why He came. The grief we face we need not face alone. Life isn't even close to fair, and death is heartache to God and man. His solutions for that are a constant presence and an eternal provision. That's also why He came. He came to cancel the curse by paying sin's penalty, thus reconciling us back to Him and to His Father, forever.

WE ARE WHY HE CAME!

Forever is real and lasts a really long time! Still, it's tough to make the heart believe forever is the main thing. But it is, and not by a little, but by a lot! That's why they call it FOREVER! There's grace for the faith to believe that.

God - help us to celebrate the lives of those we've lost, to love and value those we have, and to appreciate the lives we have to live for You. Thank you Jesus that you are Immanuel, God with us.

By the way, the two men just left Starbucks. I watched them out the window as they shared a hug and each got into their cars and drove away. Amazingly, I'm sure I saw Immanuel leave with them both, and yet here He sits, still with me. Never alone, not for one second!

NO MORE WAITING!

It's almost here! Only 2 more days! In only two days we'll celebrate one of the two most significant events in human history. (The other, is Easter) This event, that occurred over 2000 years ago, represents the moment when Immanuel "became flesh and dwelt among us" (John 1:14).

Some will debate exactly what time of year Immanuel came, or concern themselves about the exact chronology of the Christmas story. Honestly I'm not particularly concerned about either of those. I'll continue to emphasize, the big news is - He came.

Let's consider the story of the prophetess Anna.

Luke 2:36-38 (NIV) "There was also a prophet, Anna, the daughter of Penuel, of the tribe of Asher. She was very old; she had lived with her husband seven years after her marriage, and then was a widow until she was eighty-four. She never left the temple but worshiped night and day, fasting and praying. Coming up to them at that very moment, she gave thanks to God and spoke about the child to all who were looking forward to the redemption of Jerusalem."

Anna's story is one of pain, patience, and ultimately, redemption. She lost her husband after only 7 years of marriage, which likely means she spent over 60 years as a widow. "Until death do us part" came way too soon. Whatever dreams she had certainly didn't include the unpredictable and early loss of the one she loved.

Yet Anna persisted with a patient, hopeful faith, believing for the redemption of her people and her pain. Anna was born under the first covenant, the "Old Covenant." That meant waiting for redemption.

Under the Old Covenant, "God with us" meant He intervened in our circumstances, but not in our hearts. In the Old Covenant, God dwelt among people, but not in people. Under the Old Covenant He required a man-made "house to dwell in" (2 Samuel 7:5).

But Luke points out in Acts 7:48 that under the New Covenant, "The Most High does not dwell in houses made by hands…" Immanuel God with us now dwells in us. The work of redemption is an internal work with a huge external impact!

That's the work Anna and the children of Israel waited for. Sadly, some are still waiting even today. That need not be true, Christ has come. Immanuel is with us.

I understand eternity is the place of ultimate healing and restoration, and I realize the deepest hurts can cast a shadow over life lived here on earth. However, the work of redemption goes deeper still and will always shine an inexplicable light of joy on even the darkest dark.

That redemption is something we need not wait for.

It came 2000 years ago, and Anna didn't miss it, she didn't miss Immanuel. He doesn't want you or me to miss Him either. That's why He's with us. Right here, right now.

IMMANUEL, GOD WITH US - NO WAITING!

LOVE, THE GIFT THAT LASTS FOREVER

Well, we're practically there. It's Christmas Eve! Many of us have already had at least one or two dinners, opened some gifts, and the big day isn't officially until tomorrow.

If there's anything I don't like about Christmas, it's that it comes and goes too quickly! So quickly that it can feel anti-climactic. We plan and prepare, cook, and travel. We eat and open gifts, and then in a day or two Christmas is gone for another whole year.

What we celebrate at Christmas is worthy of so much more than one-day, one-week, or even one-month. Celebrations stretch from Thanksgiving to Christmas and it is a season full of busy and buying, family and feasting. I'm not suggesting we should do those all 12 months of the year.

I'm certainly not suggesting you should leave your tree up for 365 straight days, or listen to Christmas music until all your friends hate you, (I wouldn't hate you). I'm not suggesting we celebrate Christmas every day, but I am suggesting we celebrate and appreciate Christ every day. I am suggesting we remember the gifts of love and family that last from now until forever, and in fact into forever.

Love is that one gift that never ceases. Even if you've had to say good-bye to someone for now, even if that friend or family member is already with the Father, know this, the love you've shared, you STILL share. Love lasts forever, and without a gap in the middle.

LOVE ENDURES and NEVER ENDS!

1 Corinthians 13:7-8 "Love bears all things, believes all things, hopes all things, endures all things. Love never ends…"

There's one particular Christmas I remember most from when I was a kid. It had to have been around 1970, and money was definitely tight. Mom and Dad both worked and worked hard, but they also had five kids from the ages of 5 – 10. Apparently there just wasn't money for many, or any, store bought toys.

Mom, wanting to make sure we had a good Christmas, became very creative with what she had. My dad was a carpenter and often brought home scrap lumber for kindling. Mom took those scraps and from them she made me a cool little Gas Station complete with premium, regular, and unleaded pumps. To go along with my gas station she made me a truck and car, by simply drawing on square pieces of wood with magic markers. Magic indeed!

I honestly don't remember what my brothers and sisters got for Christmas that year, I was only 5 and possibly a little self-consumed. What I do remember is that we were all happy, and not because of what we got, but because of what we had.

We had a safe place of believing and belonging in Immanuel. Our home wasn't perfect, but it was permeated with the love of God, and that's a gift that lasts forever.

Immanuel, God with us, is Immanuel who gave Himself for us because He loves us, with a love that lasts forever.

MERRY CHRISTMAS!

2 Corinthians 9:15 “Thanks be to God for his inexpressible gift!”

We've spent the past 99 days emphasizing God's faithfulness to us. Now Christmas day is finally here. This particular season has been marked by pain, unthinkable pain, and yet is still filled with promise.

It’s possible that during the past year you’ve experienced personal tragedy and pain. That cannot only rob us of the joy of this season, but of life itself.

In fact, we’ve highlighted the reality that as Jesus said, "In this world you will have trouble…" (John 16:33) That's not me being negative, that's me being real. But an even greater reality is that God is with us. In fact, He also said in that same John passage, “be of good cheer, I have overcome the world.”

That's been the consistent theme of this devotional, and more importantly is the constant, unmistakable promise of God's word. He overcame by coming, and by coming, He could be with us.

That’s a prophetic promise made in Isaiah 7:15 – “All right then, the Lord himself will give you the sign. Look! The virgin will conceive a child! She will give birth to a son and will call him Immanuel (which means 'God is with us').” NLT

Christmas brings with it a reminder of that promise, and its fulfillment 2000 plus years ago. Luke 2:6-7 “While they were there, the time came for the baby to be born, and she gave birth to her firstborn, a son…”

It’s that promise that prompts us to say Merry Christmas. It isn’t perfect - no pain, no problem Christmas, but it should be a Merry Christmas.

Proverbs 17:33 says, “A joyful (merry) heart is good medicine…”

We need this season, and even more, we need that heart. We need a heart that recognizes the need for God’s presence, to appreciate His faithfulness, and to rest in His love and eternal provision. That’s good medicine!

Christmas is a reminder we need of a truth we can’t afford to forget. IMMANUEL IS GOD WITH US – Merry Christmas! (FYI, 365 days until…)

Made in the USA
Lexington, KY
29 September 2014